MEET PASTOR PETER

MEET PASTOR PETER

Studies in Peter's Second Epistle

BERNARD E. SETON

REVIEW AND HERALD PUBLISHING ASSOCIATION
Washington, DC 20039-0555
Hagerstown, MD 21740

This book was
Edited by Raymond H. Woolsey
Designed by Richard Steadham
Cover photos by Comstock, Inc. (large); David B. Sherwin (inset)
Type set: 11/12 Zapf

PRINTED IN U.S.A.

Library of Congress Cataloging in Publication Data

Seton, Bernard E., 1913-
Meet Pastor Peter.

1. Bible. N.T. Peter, 2nd—Criticism, interpretation, etc. I. Title.
BS2795.2.S47 1985 227'.9307 85-8250
ISBN 0-8280-0290-8

Contents

An Introduction

A Look at the Writer

Yes, we should like you to meet Pastor Peter.

All right. But how?

He has been dead for more than nineteen hundred years. He had little, if any, formal education. He grew up beside the Sea of Galilee in northern Palestine, where fishing would be his natural calling. It is unlikely that he originally had any other ambition than that of becoming a prosperous fisherman. International fame surely played little if any part in his dreams of the future, yet today there are very few countries where his name and his fame are not known by large numbers of people.

A few of his contemporaries came to know him very well. There was his brother Andrew, who seems to have been about as mild as Peter was bold. James and John, partners in the joint fishing business based on the Lake of Galilee, must have become well acquainted with him too. The quartet, mixed as it was, worked smoothly enough to ensure a livelihood, though prosperity may have been a long way off.

Then the young Man from Nazareth invited the four to follow Him, and they swiftly agreed. They left their boats and their nets and followed Him (see Matt. 4:18-22; Mark 1:16-20; Luke 5:1-11). Thus, although it assumed a different pattern, their partnership continued, and their names came to be known and revered beyond the northern Galilean community.

But how can we accept the invitation in our title—"Meet Pastor Peter"?

Not one of us has ever met him in the flesh. We have no way of knowing whether he was short or tall, thin or well built. Because he was a Palestinian Jew we expect him to have had dark, even black, hair, with a somewhat luxuriant beard to match. Because he was a fisherman, we take his physical strength for granted, though we may create no such virile image of his brother Andrew and his partners James and John, fellow fishermen though they all were.

There is but little doubt that our concepts in this matter of appearance are influenced by centuries of Christian art, which has interpreted the New Testament records according to the taste and convictions of each artist. It is tempting to harbor the hope that there were some simple originals from which later portraits developed. The earliest representations, crude as many of them were, molded the visions of succeeding generations. Stereotypes took shape and were so accepted that we feel almost sure we shall be able to separate Peter from among the other apostles when we meet them face to face.

If we assume, as is reasonable, that Peter and his companions were about the same age as their Leader, then our disciple also would have been about 30 years old in A.D. 27 when Jesus called him into His circle. His martyrdom is believed to have taken place in Rome in A.D. 66 or 67 when he would be about 65 to 70 years of age. At that time Paul was beheaded by a sword, while Peter was nailed to a cross. The more humane death was Paul's because he was a Roman citizen, but Peter, without that status, was treated as a common criminal and condemned to the agonies of crucifixion. Tradition maintains that he asked to suffer a still more cruel end by being transfixed head downward because he deemed himself altogether unworthy to duplicate the mode of his beloved Master's death. That decision came from a very brave and humble man. Such courage canceled any lingering memory of earlier weakness and placed Pastor Peter among the nobility of greatness.

Peter's name appears more frequently in the New Testament than that of any other of the original twelve, and is surpassed only by the later references to Saul, or Paul. In the Gospels and the first half of the Acts of the Apostles, his is the dominant human figure. But after Saul's conversion and entrance into Christian ministry, Peter becomes less prominent. There is no hint of jealousy, however. Indeed, Peter helped influence the Jerusalem Council (c. A.D. 49) into acceptance of Paul's Gentile converts as fellow Christians with the predominantly Jewish membership of the early church (see Acts 15:6-35). In relation to Paul, Peter emulated John the Baptist's attitude to Jesus: "He must increase, but I must decrease" (John 3:30).

Honored as he was with the revolutionary message "Then hath God also to the Gentiles granted repentance unto life" (Acts 11:18), Peter was unlikely to have limited his ministry to Palestine. The opening verse of the First Epistle of Peter precludes such restriction. He addressed the letter to "God's elect, strangers in the world, scattered throughout Pontus, Galatia, Cappadocia, Asia and Bithynia" (1 Peter 1:1, N.I.V.). In the first century A.D. those territories were provinces in Asia Minor; they now form part of modern Turkey. Three of the four were represented at Pentecost by Jews of the Diaspora (Acts 2:9), so it is permissible to surmise that some of those who were converted under Peter's Pentecostal preaching in Jerusalem returned to their adopted homes and spread the good news throughout those Asian territories. If so, there would be a special reason for the apostle to visit those provinces and to strengthen those believers in the faith they had accepted in the Holy Land. Later, he would continue that ministry by writing to those same people.

The personal notes that are struck in both 1 and 2 Peter persuade many commentators that the writer of those letters personally knew the main body of believers to whom the messages were addressed. This is quite possible. If Peter died in Rome about A.D. 66 or 67, he traveled far from home, and it is reasonable to conclude that, during more than three decades of Christian ministry, he visited Christian groups in Asia Minor and subsequently wrote letters to confirm them in their faith.

A Look at the Letter

We now turn to consider the evaluation placed on 2 Peter by generations of Christian leaders in postapostolic times.

Many scholars are persuaded that 1 Clement, a pastoral epistle written about A.D. 95 or 96 by an early bishop of Rome, reveals that the author was acquainted with the Second Epistle of Peter. This requires that letter to have been written prior to A.D. 95, which was only thirty years after the apostle's martyrdom—a very short space of time in comparison to the nineteen centuries that have followed. At this distance in time Bishop Clement's conclusion carries considerable weight and demolishes many arguments against Peter's authorship. Another Clement, of Alexandria (c. 150-215), is said not only to have had 2 Peter in his Bible but also to have written a commentary on that same Epistle. The theologian Origen (c. 182-251), writing around the year 240, quotes six times from 2 Peter, speaking of it as Scripture. There is also evidence that 1 and 2 Peter and Jude were widely used in Egypt during the third century (200-300). Eusebius, the "Father of Church History" (c. 260-340), classified the Second Epistle with those of James and Jude, and recognized that while some doubted their genuineness, many accepted them as authentic apostolic writings. In a festal letter dated 367, Athanasius, bishop of Alexandria in Egypt (c. 296-373), listed the books that were accepted as inspired and worthy of inclusion in the New Testament. He accepted 2 Peter while excluding the epistles of Barnabus and Clement. The Biblical scholar and translator Jerome (c. 342-420) included 2 Peter in the Vulgate, which was his Latin translation from the Hebrew, Aramaic, and Greek Scriptures. By the Council of Carthage (397) the New Testament canon, or books accepted as inspired, was settled to the satisfaction of orthodox believers, and included 2 Peter as a genuine apostolic writing.

A comparison of the two Epistles that bear Peter's name produces strong support for his authorship of both, while allowing for differences arising from differing circumstances, differing needs, and possibly different scribes. Those differences are more apparent in the Greek text than in the many translations of the two Epistles. The writing in the first letter is on a higher literary plane; the second is more flowery and contains more Hebrew expressions. The latter also reveals an Aramaic cast of thought, overlaid with an Asiatic style of writing that is thought to have been peculiar to Asia Minor just prior to the Christian Era. This might have come from the scribe who translated Peter's Aramaic into that style of Greek. Peter himself says Silvanus was his scribe for the First Epistle (1 Peter 5:12), but no individual is named for the Second. If a scribe other than Silvanus was used for the second letter, that would adequately explain the difference in style between the two writings.

We should also allow for the differing subject matter. First Peter seeks to fortify believers in anticipation of persecution (chap. 4:12), while 2 Peter encourages them to be faithful in anticipation of their Lord's return (chap.

3:9-14). Any other differences should be regarded as complementary rather than contradictory—that is, each letter adds to the instruction given by the other.

A study of the language and thought patterns in the two letters, and comparisons with Peter's sermons in Acts 1-5 and 10, reveal close similarities in style, even to the use of words employed elsewhere only by Peter in his speeches as recorded in the book of Acts. The likeness appears all the more impressive when it is contrasted with the obvious stylistic differences between the two New Testament letters and the rejected Apocalypse of Peter, which so largely depends on the substance of 2 Peter. Confirmation of the similarities in the two canonical books comes from a computerized comparison of the language used in the two Epistles: they are similar enough to each other to establish their common authorship, yet together they are different from other New Testament books. A similar comparison, with or without computer, can be made with 1 Timothy and Titus, each of which is widely accepted as Pauline.

It is probable that the original of 2 Peter, sent to a central church or to a principal group of believers, was copied and distributed to nearby Christian groups who in turn would make further copies and send them to more distant congregations until all in the designated areas would have a copy of Peter's message. The fact that such a letter survived reflects the honor in which the apostle's message was held. Its recipients treasured the message that came from one of their Lord's first disciples!

Fortified by this brief examination of the Epistle's credentials, and profiting from its counsels, we can keep company with its first readers. Its very brevity, as compared with many other New Testament letters, should make it easier for us to grasp and apply its messages to our own circumstances. Faithful study of its sixty-one verses, and consideration of their relationship to Jude's still briefer Epistle, cannot but enrich our faith and fortify our resolve to follow the same Lord whom the mature Peter so nobly served. Before embarking on such study, should we not admit deep gratitude for the letter's preservation? Thousands, even millions, of other contemporary writings have been lost: This one, with its New Testament companions, has been saved!

Those who desire more detailed aid, of a thoroughly reliable nature and deeply spiritual in content, can find it, at a very modest cost, in *The Second Epistle of Peter and the Epistle of Jude,* by Michael Green, M.A., B.D., in the Tyndale New Testament Commentaries, published by William B. Eerdmans Publishing Company, Grand Rapids, Michigan, 1968.

Writer and Readers

(2 Peter 1:1-4)

The Writer

In the case of most New Testament letters there is no need to turn to their concluding paragraphs to discover the identity of their writers. With the exception of the Epistle to the Hebrews and the three general Epistles of John, that information appears as the first word in the first sentence of each letter. Peter's First Epistle follows the general pattern. The second letter differs slightly by using a double name, Simon Peter.

The apostle's use of his two names may have been, consciously or otherwise, an embracing of his whole life just prior to his death. His childhood Hebrew name was *Shimeon,* first used in the Old Testament for the second son of Jacob and Leah (Gen. 29:33), and signifying "hearing with acceptance." In first-century Palestine, especially in Galilee where there was a strong Greek-speaking element, it would often be expressed in its Greek form of *Symeon,* from which we derive the name *Simon.* For fuller identification, especially in Jewish circles, the bearer would be known by the Aramaic form, Simon Bar-Jona, that is, Simon son of John.

Simon's discipleship with Jesus of Nazareth brought him yet another name. When he first came face to face with Jesus he heard the words: "Thou art Simon the son of Jona: thou shalt be called Cephas" (John 1:42). The Lord used the Aramaic word *Kêpha',* which passes into Greek as *Kephas* and is anglicized into *Cephas*. Each of these forms holds the original meaning of "stone." Oscar Cullman, a Swiss theologian, has suggested that Simon Peter might today be rendered as "Simon Rock" (or "Stone"), giving him first and second names as is currently the custom in Western societies.

Later, the disciple made his magnificent declaration, "Thou art the Christ, the Son of the living God" (Matt. 16:16). Christ then called him "blessed," and stated, "Thou art Peter," reminding him of the special name He had bestowed upon him at his initial call. This time the Saviour dwelt on the significance of the Aramaic word that Matthew translates into the Greek *petros*, "a stone." This is then set against the Greek *petra*, a feminine form signifying "a rock." In this way, the Master differentiated between the disciple and the church that He Himself was building on His own person and office. It was inconceivable, then, that the disciple would ever forget the significance of his own startling confession or of the name that was confirmed because of it. Every mention of the name *Peter* would be liable to remind him of the occasion when the Master confirmed the name for him.

The New Testament use of the variant forms of the apostle's names reveals no sudden irreversible change from the earlier to the later. Simon, or Simon called Peter, or Simon Peter occurs at frequent intervals in each Gospel. The simple form, Peter, appears both early and late, but with increasing frequency after the initial call to discipleship. In Acts the preferences are almost entirely for Peter. In 1 Peter the apostle refers to himself as Peter, but in 2 Peter he introduces himself as Simon Peter. If the two letters were addressed to the same readership, there would seem to be no obvious significance in the use of one form as against the other. In the Greco-Roman world of Asia Minor, the name *Peter* may have been more readily recognized, but the Jewish/Gentile mixture of *Simon*

Peter might have had some appeal to the expatriate Jewish Christians to whom the second letter was probably addressed.

Of Peter's childhood nothing is now known. It must have been typical of the Jewish boys of his day, modified only by family finances. Life in Roman-occupied Galilee served as a tough school for any youngster. Indeed, an onlooker might have been tempted to ask, "Can any good thing come out of Galilee?" The unequivocal answer must be "Yes!" There came James and John, Andrew—and Peter! To say nothing of One who chose to be reared in that province! If it is true, as the poet George W. Russell (alias "AE") claims, that "in the lost boyhood of Judas, Christ was betrayed" (and how tragically true that proved to be), then how satisfyingly right it is that in Simon's formative youth Christ was glorified!

From the apostle John we learn that Simon's hometown was Bethsaida, which signified "house of fishing." This village or town is often identified as Bethsaida Julias, a town that stood on the northern shore of the Lake of Galilee, to the east of where the river Jordan enters the lake. But there is another claimant for the honor of being the home of Philip, Andrew, and Peter. Mark tells us that shortly after Jesus called Andrew and Simon, James and John, the group moved from the lakeside into Capernaum. There, on the Sabbath, Jesus taught in the synagogue. Then He went "forthwith" into the home of Simon and Andrew and there healed Simon's mother-in-law of whatever sickness (possibly malaria) was troubling her (Mark 1:14-31). This is difficult to reconcile with John's clear statement that Bethsaida was home for Philip, Simon, and Andrew, unless their Bethsaida is identified as the small fishing village that lay adjacent to Capernaum and served it as port. This seems preferable to the other town, which would have taken longer to reach (see verse 29).

The reference to Simon's mother-in-law provides the only information we have concerning the marital state of any of the twelve disciples. It is corroborated by Paul's somewhat plaintive question in 1 Corinthians 9:5, which indicates that Cephas (Simon Peter) was sometimes accompanied by his wife on his missionary journeys, as were "other apostles." Peter is the only one of the twelve, however, who is specifically shown to be married. It will be very interesting to hear Mrs. Peter's story when, at the first resurrection, she is reunited with her husband!

Having identified himself, the writer presents his credentials. What a story he *could* have told! But how modest and self-effacing is the reference to himself! The Greek word *doulos,* here translated "servant," originally applied to one who was born into slavery, in contrast to the unfortunate taken captive in war and enslaved by the victorious party. In Christian terminology there was no such enslavement. The convert's only compulsion came from a grateful love for the One who had redeemed him from bondage to sin. He willingly gave himself to that Redeemer, rendering voluntary service out of a thankful heart.

Such a servant was Peter. What a contrast to the man who, some thirty-five years before, had taken the first step into discipleship. Jesus had just been baptized and given public recognition by John the Baptist. John's testimony led two of his own disciples, Andrew and John, to follow Jesus. Andrew's first act under his new allegiance was to bring his own brother Simon to Jesus. The young preacher appraised the new recruit's character and, on the spot, gave him a new name. Simon became Peter, the latter being used far more frequently than his birth-name (John 1:35-42).

More than a year later, probably in the spring of A.D. 29, soon after Jesus began His Galilean ministry, He made a second, definitive call. Peter, his brother Andrew, and their friends James and John "straightway left their nets, and followed him" (Matt. 4:20). Some months later the Master appointed twelve of His followers to be with Him in His expanding ministry. Simon Peter's name comes first (Matt. 10:2-4; Mark 3:16-19; Luke 6:14-16; Acts 1:13). That position is justified by the leading role played by its bearer, though he is given no title of preeminence in the Gospels or in the book of Acts. But a glance through the four narratives quickly pinpoints the prominence of Peter among his fellow disciples. His was the boat from which Jesus "taught the people" (Luke 5:1-3). His was the net that miraculously filled with fish (verses 4-7). His was the voice that confessed: "I am a sinful man, O Lord" (verse 8).

It was Peter who, in the region of Caesarea Philippi beyond the northern borders of Galilee, recognized and acknowledged Jesus as "the Christ, the Son of the living God" (Matt. 16:16), and received from his Master's lips the accolade "Blessed art thou, Simon Bar-jona. . . . Upon this rock [of belief in Jesus as Christ] I will build my church" (verses 17, 18). It was Peter who later had the temerity to urge his Lord to flee from martyrdom (verse 22).

"Six days later Jesus took Peter, James, and John . . . , and led them up a high mountain where they were alone; and in their presence he was transfigured" (Matt. 17:1, 2, N.E.B.). On that mountain, the trio, with Peter at the head, was granted the closest and most vivid glimpse of Divinity ever granted to mortal men. Small wonder that after the passage of more than thirty years the apostle still clearly recalled that revelation, and shared its awesome wonder with men and women in a far-off land!

As the Perfect Life taught His disciples the unforgettable lesson of humility through the washing of their feet, "Simon Peter saith unto him, Lord, not my feet only, but also my hands and my head" (John 13:9). In Gethsemane an hour or two later the same disciple used a sword in his Master's defense and cut off an opponent's ear (chap.

18:10), yet soon joined his companions as they forsook Christ and fled (Matt. 26:56). Unlike his fellows, he then trailed his captive Leader "afar off unto the high priest's palace, . . . to see the end" (verse 58). Yet in the early-morning hours that followed, it was the same man who, when challenged whether he was not also one of Jesus' associates, began "to curse and to swear, saying, I know not the man." Almost immediately remorse overtook him, "and he went out, and wept bitterly" (verses 74, 75).

His earlier brave words and firm resolves were undone. In spite of his desire to be bold and faithful, he found himself no stronger than nine of his companions, different only in degree from Judas, and far below John in his nearness to his Lord. He had maneuvered himself into a situation he was not strong enough to dominate. In that bitter hour of self-hatred he must have plumbed the depths of despair and defeat. Yet he may have begun the climb out of that self-made slough of despond by recalling the optimistic words that Jesus had spoken about thirty hours beforehand: "I have prayed for thee, that thy faith fail not: and when thou art converted, strengthen thy brethren" (Luke 22:32). In spite of his heinous denial, all was not lost. His Leader believed in him and his future. There was time to redeem the temporary cowardice and to demonstrate his complete loyalty, even unto death, to the One whom he so ardently loved.

Calvary and its resurrection sequel were the transforming events for Peter. "Greater love hath no man than this, that a man lay down his life for his friends," Jesus had said (John 15:13), and Peter saw Him make that sacrifice. It might have been the end of all his hopes. The Sabbath that followed the crucifixion was an indescribably sad, muted one. "We trusted that it had been he which should have redeemed Israel" (Luke 24:21). But when Sunday morning was about to dawn and Mary Magdalene ran back from the tomb to tell Peter and John that their Lord had disappeared from the grave, Peter dashed out, with John hard on his heels, to find what had happened to their Master. Although John was the first to reach the grave site, Peter was first into the sepulcher. He found it empty and felt the first glimmer of hope (John 20:1-10). A little later that same day, after the revelation at Emmaus (Luke 24:13-32), the Lord personally appeared to Simon before making Himself known to the larger group (verses 34, 36-43). Judas was dead. Peter qualified as being the one most in need of encouragement, so his Lord singled him out for that special face-to-face postresurrection encounter that wiped out the shame of denial and set the impulsive one's feet on the road to faithful, confident leadership.

What a change those years of association with Christ had brought! The fisherman had become a disciple: The disciple had developed into an apostle. The young man who seemed indentured for life to a fisherman's partnership had taken service with the Son of God. God's Son had only three and a half years for formal public service on earth. The apostle was to have three and a half decades!

It was in Jerusalem that Peter tried his first apostolic steps. Under the Spirit's direction, he and his eleven companions left the house where the Comforter had come upon them, went into the city, and began to proclaim that Jesus of Nazareth was the Saviour of mankind. Quickly "the multitude came together, and were confounded, because that every man heard them speak in his own language," or dialect (Acts 2:6). The mantle of leadership, practical if not titular, seemed to fall on Peter's shoulders. "Standing up with the eleven," he boldly preached that "God hath made that same Jesus, whom ye have crucified, both Lord and Christ" (verses 14, 36). From that day his was the leading voice, ably accompanied by John's, that preached to the listening multitudes and to the hostile authorities (chaps. 2:38; 3:1-11, 12-26; 4:8-12, 19-21). His was the authority that handled the sorry case of Ananias and Sapphira (chap. 5:1-11). His shadow was credited with having healing power (verses 12-26). His voice, supported by those of his colleagues, declared: "We ought to obey God rather than men" (verse 29). With John—they formed a powerful partnership—he was appointed to organize the converts garnered from Philip's preaching in Samaria, and to introduce them to the Holy Spirit's leadership (chap. 8:5-8, 14-17). Peter also had to handle the mercenary approach of Simon Magus to spirit possession (verses 9-13, 18-24). After Saul's conversion (chap. 9:1-30) and the respite that came to the persecuted infant church (verse 32), Peter went still further afield, visiting groups at Lydda (modern Lod, with its international airport), Joppa (Jaffa, merging into Tel Aviv), and northward to Caesarea (chap. 10:1-48), where he learned that "God [hath] also to the Gentiles granted repentance unto life" (chap. 11:18).

Some three years after Saul's baptism, he, according to his own account, "went up to Jerusalem to see Peter, and abode with him fifteen days" (Gal. 1:18). The only other apostle mentioned is James, the Lord's brother (verse 19), so it would appear that Peter held a prominent position in church leadership at that time. We later find him attending the first church council, held in Jerusalem, probably in A.D. 49, where the apostle James served as chairman (Acts 15:1-21). The need for such a gathering arose from the influx of Gentiles into the hitherto largely Jewish church. Peter's report of the instructive vision that had come to him led chairman James to announce the liberating decision that opened the doors of the church to Gentile believers without their being subject to Jewish rituals (verse 19, 20). In delivering that decision, James referred to Peter as Symeon or Simon (verse 14)—the only clear occasion when the original Greek form of the apostle's name occurs in the New Testament, apart from its possible use at the opening of Peter's own Second Epistle.

But more important than spelling is the evidence of Peter's being wholeheartedly committed to sharing the gospel with the Gentiles. He was completely ready to welcome them into Christian fellowship without burdensome and unnecessary rites. This background to his ministry lends credence to his serving both Jew and Gentile in person and through pastoral letters.

As his pastoral experience developed, Paul sought to discourage his converts from rendering allegiance to men instead of to Christ. (See Acts 18:1-6 and 1 Cor. 1:12-15.) He deliberately turns them away from himself, and from Apollos, and from *Cephas*. Now Paul was the evangelist who founded the Corinthian church during a stay of eighteen months in that seaport city (Acts 18:7-11). Apollos, a learned Jew from Alexandria, also served the Lord in the same city (verses 24-28). It seems highly probable, therefore, that Cephas (Peter) also had contributed to the Corinthians' spiritual growth, otherwise there would have been no point in Paul's naming him with Apollos and himself. There is, then, the possibility that our apostle had traveled far from Jerusalem even in those earlier years, and could have passed through Asia Minor into Greece, ministering to infant Christian communities, founding others, and constantly contributing to the church's growth.

The Readers

How remarkable that a letter written almost two millenniums ago, and without its writer having any inkling that it would form a part of the unforeseen New Testament, should prove so helpful to Christians of every race and language and century! The very anonymity of the recipients permits us now to accept that message as addressed to ourselves.

The opening phrase of 2 Peter, "to them that have obtained like precious faith with us," is timeless and placeless: it is of universal application. "Faith," in this setting, is susceptible of at least two interpretations. It can be a direct reference to the Christian faith or religion. Or it can refer to that quality by which we grasp eternal truths that are normally beyond the reach of human beings and by which we trust God for our salvation. The first explanation seems more meaningful here, though we should also leave room for the second.

The writer makes no attempt to place himself on a higher plane than his readers. There are no hierarchies among the redeemed. "There is none righteous, no, not one" (Rom. 3:10). All have sinned, and all are dependent on grace for salvation. This universal need is met by a universal solution, which both writer and readers have already utilized. They have obtained, or "there has been allotted" (2 Peter 1:1, Weymouth), at no credit to themselves, the same kind of redemption granted to Peter and his companions. The writer had no doubts on that score, for at the very beginning of his ministry he had boldly declared before Annas and Caiaphas: "Salvation is found in no one else, for there is no other name under heaven given to men by which we must be saved" (Acts 4:12, N.I.V.). And this salvation functions not by God's turning a blind eye to our sins, for that would be an unrighteous act. It operates through our acceptance of and belief in the impeccable rightness or justice of the One who is both our God and our Saviour from sin, that is, Christ. That interpretation of the phrase "God and our Saviour Jesus Christ" (2 Peter 1:1, K.J.V.) conveys the significance of the original wording. It discloses the apostle's unshaken conviction that the Lord, with whom he had lived for three and one-half years, is both his God and Saviour, and theirs to whom he was writing. With Thomas, who had been the doubter, he confesses concerning his Master: "My Lord and my God" (John 20:28; cf. Acts 2:36; 5:31).

The initial salutation (2 Peter 1:1) looks back to the past, dwelling on what Christ has already done for us. In verse 2 the writer looks forward, expressing the wish that the gifts of grace and peace might be multiplied on a continuing basis. The initial bestowal of such qualities comes with the acceptance of Christ as Saviour, but that is not the end. The original qualities are to be *multiplied* or increased, not automatically, not soul-lessly, but by a spiritual process whereby they grow.

"Grace" (Greek *charis*) is one of the New Testament's great words. It does not appear in Matthew or Mark; Luke employs it once in his Gospel (chap. 2:40); John uses it three times, all in chapter one with reference to the Word (verses 14, 16, 17); Luke makes use of it ten times in Acts. But it is Paul who brings the term into greatest prominence, employing it more than ninety times in his fourteen Epistles, mostly with reference to the moral quality exercised by the Godhead for mankind's salvation, but also seeing it functioning in the lives of Christians.

Peter here views grace as the fruitage of spiritual education, and prays that his readers might acquire increased stocks of the gift. He links it with peace (Greek *eirēnē,* from which we form the name *Irene*). This is not just an absence of strife, though that meaning is included, but is a gift from God, a positive quality that flows from a Christian's religion, being built into his character, providing the setting in which other fruits of the Spirit can flourish.

Peter does more than pray that his friends might receive the gifts. He tells them how those desirable qualities may be obtained. They come "through [or *in*] the knowledge of God, and of Jesus our Lord" (chap. 1:2). It is tempting to emphasize the word used here for "knowledge" *(epignōsis)*. In the New Testament it often refers to an understanding that is based on personal experience. In Paul's writings it lifts the reader out of secular into spiritual realms. Peter's thought undoubtedly moves in similar channels, for he is speaking of the "knowledge of God." But our interpretation of that phrase must be tempered by recalling that the closing words of this Epistle (chap. 3:18) do not employ *epignōsis* but choose the more common and less intensive word for knowledge, *gnōsis*, as the writer urges us to "grow in grace, and in the *knowledge* of our Lord and Saviour Jesus Christ." Here, if anywhere, he or his scribe would surely have used the richer word if he had intended to emphasize the intensive quality of the personal knowledge of Jesus that Christians are to cultivate. This he did not do, so we should refrain from overstressing his use of *epignōsis* here in verse 2. At the same time, let us acknowledge our need to increase our understanding of and our personal, experiential acquaintance with God and with Jesus, noting that both the Father and the Son are mentioned here.

In verse 3 we learn that all gifts "that pertain unto life and godliness" are given to us by Jesus, the One who is the last-mentioned at the close of verse 2. Just as He breathed into Adam the breath of life to make him a living soul, so will the Creator give us all the power that we need for life and Godlikeness. We should not wait for some earth-shattering event to propel us into godly living—every needful power is already available to us, and will operate in us if only we permit those powers to function. That will happen as we increase our personal knowledge of Him who, by the pure radiance of His own winsome ministry and sinless life, draws us unto Himself.

Peter is here speaking from personal experience. He had caught an early glimpse of his Master's glory in the miraculous draft of fishes in the Lake of Gennesaret. This drew from him the admission "I am a sinful man, O Lord," and led to his becoming a full-time follower of the young Preacher (Luke 5:1-11). The mature apostle now suggests that a comparable encounter will reveal Christ's glory to all who permit His divine power to operate in their lives. This revelation will stimulate us to aspire to His "glory" which derives from His sinlessness, and His "virtue" or goodness, His perfection of character.

In the original there is no division between verses 3 and 4. The "whereby" or "by which" in verse 4 refers to the thoughts in verse 3, particularly "his divine power" and "the knowledge of him." The divine perfections of Father and Son, there being no distinction between the two in this respect, make available to all Their children every endowment necessary for salvation. These gifts are displayed, as jewels on a velvet cushion, in the "exceeding great and precious promises" that have already been given and await only our acceptance and employment.

Peter doubtless had in mind those promises recorded in the Old Testament and those given by the Master during His brief ministry in Palestine. These would include those given in Genesis 3:15; Exodus 15:26; Deuteronomy 33:27; Job 19:25, 26; Psalms 23; 34:19; 91:1; Isaiah 9:6,7; 26:3; 55:6, 7; Jeremiah 31:33, 34; Daniel 2:44; Matthew 1:21; 16:27; 28:19, 20; John 6:35; 10:10, 11, 16. To these we can add those that came later through the writings of Paul, James, John, Jude, and Peter himself. As we compile our own lists, and as we personally discover how reliable they are, we too shall be able to speak convincingly of "exceeding great and precious promises."

But we need to do more than speak about the inspired assurances: We must live lives that are consistent with the realities of those promises. Through them, we must become "partakers of [or "sharers in"] the divine nature" (2 Peter 1:4). This is an amazing concept, but one that is in complete harmony with other New Testament ideals such as are given in John 1:12; Romans 5:1, 2; 2 Corinthians 5:17; 1 John 3:2. Acceptance of these inspired visions will stimulate us to reach up to their high standards, to lay hold of the divine power that Christ has made available to us until, with other saints, we "come to share in the very being of God" (verse 4, N.E.B.). The mind of Christ must replace the promptings of our carnal natures until, as Edwin Hatch so beautifully suggests in his hymn "Breathe on me, Breath of God," we truthfully pray:

"That I may love what Thou dost love,
And do what Thou wouldst do."

Such aspirations are not natural to humans. To realize them we must deliberately turn our backs on "the corruption that is in the world through lust." That, let us admit, takes some doing, for the world in which we live is full of moral corruption, depravity, horrific kinds of wickedness, all of which are implied in the one word "corruption." To escape such evils we must flee from them, as Peter suggests by the word translated "escape." He uses an emphatic form, employed only by him in the New Testament (verse 4; chap. 2:18, 20). His word suggests "flight from." This involves no cowardice. It is the application of Christian common sense. It is the most effective way of escaping the "lusts of the flesh" (verse 18), the moral pollution, the enslaving habits that degrade the image of God in men and women. The best defense against such evils is flight from them; which will enable us to "escape the corruption." We need feel no shame in running away from evil, but for self-defense should remember the truth of Alexander Pope's words:

Vice is a monster of so frightful mien,
As to be hated needs but to be seen;
Yet seen too oft, familiar with her face,
We first endure, then pity, then embrace.

Pastor Peter's Counsel

(2 Peter 1:5-11)

In the opening paragraph of Peter's second letter (chap. 1:1-4) the loving and lovable leader has greeted his readers and focused their attention on the Godhead's ambition for each of them. The Father and the Son (the Holy Ghost is named later, in verse 21) want to see, inconceivable as it may first appear to be, Their earthly subjects become sharers in Their divine nature. What could motivate such a wish? There is only one credible answer: The Creators love Their creation. They are the prototypes reflected very, very faintly in the ideal marriage where husband and wife come together in a holy act to create another new life as the supreme expression of their love.

This concept is the backdrop against which Paul paints his picture of the ideal marriage (Eph. 5:22-30). It is what prompted him to reach the astounding conclusion: "Christ also loved the church, and gave himself for it; . . . that he might present it to himself" as a glorious, sinless, holy church (verses 25-27). Since Eden, Christ had longed for the re-creation of His subjects in the image of God—"In love he predestined us to be adopted as his sons through Jesus Christ" (chap. 1:4, N.I.V.). A vital part of that adoption is the implanting of the divine character in each of the redeemed, man and woman, boy and girl. In that way, all who accept Him as their Saviour become "partakers of the divine nature."

Peter sees the fulfillment of that divine vision being initiated during the Christian's earthly life. The convert has turned from "the corruption that is in the world." His mind is set in the right direction. All will be well if he continues on that road. He must not stand still; he must make spiritual progress. He must continue to add to the spiritual equipment that came with conversion (2 Peter 1:5). Such development is not optional; rather, it is obligatory, as is made clear in contemporary translations, "for this very reason" (R.S.V., N.I.V.), and by words that imply "hastening," "exerting oneself," "adding to," or "eagerly seeking."

At the close of his Epistle the apostle summarizes such progress as growth in grace (chap. 3:18). Here he itemizes the development, listing seven or eight qualities that should be built into every Christian's character. He appears to take the believer's possession of the first trait, "faith," for granted, possibly seeing it as the foundation on which the other seven are listed. This attitude harmonizes with that of the author of Hebrews, who states that "without faith it is impossible to please him [God]: for he that cometh to God must believe that he is" (Heb. 11:6). Room must also be preserved for viewing the expression "your faith" in verse 5 of our chapter as a simple reference to the readers' religion (compare to verse 1). When that foundational disposition is secured, attention can then be given to other gifts. This would make "virtue" the first of the seven rungs in "Peter's ladder."

There are two schools of thought as to the significance of the order in which those "rungs" are listed, except "charity" or love, which is placed last, as it is in Paul's classic exposition in 1 Corinthians 13:13. Some commentators may see more significance than the author himself intended when he wrote the passage.

After faith comes "virtue" *(aretē)*, a term that has

already appeared at the end of verse 3, where it refers to one of our Lord's qualities that inspire us to follow Him. Here it may be rendered as "excellence," with reference to our own characters or dispositions, suggesting that faith should yield some verifiable improvement in our conduct. Virtue, in turn, is to be accompanied by "knowledge." The reference is to basic knowledge *(gnōsis)*, rather than to the more specialized *epignōsis* (see under verse 2). All Christians should increase their store of such knowledge, specifically in that which is morally sound, that will make them "wise unto salvation" (2 Tim. 3:15). And the pastor has in mind the highest knowledge of all—that personal acquaintance, in the deepest possible sense of the term, with the Father and with the Son. That is his continuing concern in this letter. He reveals it in 2 Peter 1:2, where he expresses the wish that his readers might obtain the knowledge *(epignōsis)* of God and of Christ that will increase their supply of grace and peace. In verse 3 that experiential knowledge of Christ is said to bring us all that we need for eternal life, while in verse 8 the same kind of knowledge is said to make us fertile and fruitful. No less valuable is its function as recorded in chapter 2:20, where the early Christians are said to escape "the pollutions of the world through the knowledge of the Lord and Saviour Jesus Christ." What rewards await those who add an intimate acquaintance with their Redeemer to the moral excellence that should follow hard on the heels of faith!

The spiritual addition continues with the introduction of "temperance." The original word *(eğkrateia)* for this fourth "rung" of the ladder may be translated more accurately as "self-control." Its central concept is strength that is exercised over one's self in discipline similar to that exerted by contestants in the Greek games. Rigorous self-denial in respect of food, drink, exercise, and pleasure was maintained for ten months prior to those games. The entrants did it for fleeting fame and a quickly fading circlet of laurel leaves. We are called to a permanent program of self-denial as preparation for sharing in the divine nature (see 1 Cor. 9:24-27). So many of our habits stem from our all-too-frail humanity. Many of them must be shed if we are to attain to the sonship and daughterhood to which God is calling us. Temperance as abstention from alcoholic drink, control of other drinking and eating habits, balance in programs of work and play, choice of recreation, our use of time—all are involved in the contributions we ourselves can make toward Godlikeness. And lest that should sound like salvation by works, let us remember that temperance or self-control is a fruit of the Spirit (Gal. 5:22, 23), and we may count on the Spirit's aid in our struggles against human frailties.

Some will apply the next virtue, "patience," to theological situations, seeing it as "perseverance," "endurance," or "fortitude" exercised during our Christian pilgrimage. Few will deny our daily need of the commodity. Life provides innumerable situations that call for forbearance. Our fellow travelers furnish us frequent occasions to use whatever stocks of patience we possess, and we in turn provide them with innumerable opportunities for exercise of similar tolerance. Babies, children, husbands, wives, neighbors, workmates, colleagues, the elderly—how generously they enable us to develop this supplement to our faith! In addition, those who relate closely to the three angels' messages in Revelation 14:6-12 will anticipate their need for sizable stores of the gift, for they are expected to possess and to exercise "the patience of the saints"! Let us remember that "the God of patience" (Rom. 15:5) is able and ready to furnish us with all we need of that commodity!

We have already met the next virtue in verse 3, but its significance will stand closer investigation than we gave it earlier. "Godliness" is used as a translation of the Greek word *eusebeia,* which, in pagan circles, conveyed the idea of "reverence" or "piety" in relation to pagan gods. In the New Testament the term occurs fifteen times, being used by Peter in this second letter and in Paul's pastoral Epistles (1 and 2 Timothy and Titus). It there refers to the believer's complete lifestyle, which should reflect his humble, adoring, reverent relationship to the Godhead, not only in his formal acts of worship but in his daily conduct. In that sense it is correctly rendered as "godliness" or "Godlikeness," which sets a very high standard indeed.

Next, the apostle turns to our conduct toward our fellowmen. That, he says, should be governed by "brotherly kindness," or, more literally, "brotherly love" (*philadelphia* in the Greek). The juxtaposition of godliness with brotherly love is no accident. It serves to cover the whole duty of man—his relation to God and to his fellow human beings. It harmonizes with Moses' and Christ's summary of the royal law, which should govern our relationships with our Maker and our neighbors. Paul reminds us that "love is the fulfilling of the law" (Rom. 13:10), James stresses our need to love our neighbor as ourselves (chap. 2:9), and Peter here makes brotherly and sisterly love an essential component of true religion.

Love for our neighbors is a big stride on our way to love for our God, which is the final rung on Peter's ladder. The quality of that love is not open to question. The writer settles it by his use of the word *agape,* the word that Paul so peerlessly expounds in 1 Corinthians 13. Peter's use of it here, and John's employment of it in recording the Master's postresurrection dialogue with Peter (John 21:15-17), emphasize the lofty nature of that "charity," or "love," and convey to us our need to cultivate that holy love for God and that selfless love for our neighbors as Jesus Himself taught us (Matt. 22:34-40; Luke 10:25-27).

When that twofold affection is attained we shall have safely and successfully climbed to the top of the ladder that the apostle has seen as the connector between earth and heaven.

Such assurance finds justification in the sentence (verse 8) that follows the reference to "charity," or "love." To those who possess and develop the eight recommended qualities, the writer promises fruitful employment, for they will be neither idle nor fruitless. This develops from their personal knowledge *(epignōsis)* of Jesus. It seems that the apostle cannot get away from an awareness of their need to know their Lord intimately. He sees that as the heart of their Christian experience, as indeed it must be of ours. If that is lacking, the professing Christian is virtually blind or, at the best, *myopic,* or shortsighted (verse 9). He must be clinging to his old sins, forgetting that, through repentance and baptism, he has already been cleansed. We must continually remind ourselves of what Christ has done for us at our conversion. Failure to remember the reality of such redemption can be fatal. We need good memories!

Now comes the positive Peter! Be it far from him to leave his "brethren," his fellow believers, his readers, floundering in doubt derived from forgetfulness. Oh no! They are "diligently" to revitalize their response to the original call that had led them from heathenism or Judaism into the disciplined freedom of Christianity (verse 10). We should follow a similar program, for our memories are also short; we need to recall the time and the circumstances of God's call to us. We do well to remind ourselves of our "election." There is no hint of predestination here: God elects all men to be saved. As the apostle makes so clear in his third chapter, "the Lord is . . . not willing that any should perish" (verse 9), and has already done all that is necessary for all to be saved. But He does not force salvation on anyone. Salvation is freely offered; it must be freely received. In need of redemption, we must reach up for the proffered gift of eternal life. Those who accept are "the elect" who have made their calling and election sure. They shall never "fall," that is, "stumble," or as one version expresses it, "come to grief" (chap. 1:10, N.E.B.). This is not teaching present perfectionism, nor "once saved, always saved." Peter's intent is to encourage Christians to keep bright the memories of their response to God's earlier call, and to do this most diligently. In a still more comprehensive interpretation we can relate "do these things" to the qualities that comprise "the ladder" (verse 5-7, 8 and 9, as well as 10). The habitual practice of the listed Christian virtues will keep our feet on the way of salvation and prevent our slipping back into habitual sin.

Verse 11 continues the admonition begun in verse 10, and depicts the benefit that will be reaped by fostering a personal knowledge of *our* Lord and Saviour Jesus Christ. Such care will help to make our calling and election sure. Faithful pursuance of the divine program, which includes complete trust in our Saviour for our salvation, will bring us into "the everlasting kingdom." That this is not accomplished by our own efforts is made clear by the phrase "shall be ministered," which shows that it is given to us by a power outside of ourselves.

As we have come to expect, but should never take for granted, that "entrance" (*eisodos,* the reverse of *exodus*) will be on a lavish scale. The word translated "abundantly" is literally rendered "richly"—no aspect of the welcome will be skimped; its generosity will amaze us. Our surprise and gratitude will continue into eternity, for we shall then be citizens not merely of an everlasting kingdom, but of an eternal kingdom that has many other amazing features in addition to its timeless duration. The chiefest of those is its belonging to "our Lord and Saviour Jesus Christ," who is Himself eternal.

Journey's End

(2 Peter 1:11-15)

It is apparent, even from a cursory reading of 2 Peter 1:12, that the apostle was acutely conscious of a responsibility toward the congregations who would read his letter or hear it read to them. Anticipation of the coming of the eternal kingdom (verse 11) made it impossible for him to refrain from reminding them of the gospel's verities, even though he realized they were well acquainted with them and knew the relation of doctrine to their daily lives. They were firmly grounded in "present truth," that is, the body of teaching they had received from their teachers, or even from Peter himself, and which was especially relevant to their circumstances. Nevertheless, they needed, as we all do, to be freshly reminded of the foundations of their faith. He wanted to discharge that duty most faithfully while life was granted to him (verse 13). We are justified, therefore, in concluding that the prime purpose of the Epistle was to refresh the believers' grasp of the gospel and to encourage them to apply its precepts to the lives they were to lead in the second half of that first century.

In such a context it is interesting to note that Peter uses the same word, translated "tabernacle," as John employed in his Gospel when he recorded that "the Word was made flesh, and dwelt [or "tabernacled"] among us" (chap. 1:14). Awareness of his approaching death made Peter sensitive to the transitory nature of human life (compare Ps. 103:15, 16). His own would soon be over, and from that perspective it seemed little more than a brief stay in a tent. During the little time remaining to him he wanted to arouse the congregations in Asia Minor to remember the principal tenets of their religion. He does not specifically list those tenets at this juncture, but we find them scattered throughout the remainder of the Epistle. Who is there, among present-day Christians, who does not need stirring up, being put in remembrance of the foundations of his or her faith? With but little adjustment, we may well pray Rudyard Kipling's prayer:

Lord God of hosts, be with us yet,
Lest we forget, lest we forget.

We should also recall the well-used dictum "We have nothing to fear for the future, except as we shall forget the way the Lord has led us, and His teaching in our past history."—*Life Sketches,* p. 196. Blessed are we if we have good memories to recall God's mercies and His directives!

The apostle wrote under divine compulsion, for he knew that his available time and opportunities to encourage them were few. His sands of time were running out (verse 14). Had he lived in a later age he could have poignantly quoted Andrew Marvell's prescient words:

But at my back I always hear
Time's wingèd chariot hurrying near.

But he had no need of external reminders. Could he ever forget his Lord's postresurrection revelation of the way his own life's end would come? Poor would be the memory that could not recall every one of those solemn words! " 'I tell you this in very truth: when you were young you fastened your belt about you and walked where you chose; but when you are old you will stretch out your arms, and a stranger will bind you fast, and carry you where you have no wish to go.' " Maybe he had overheard John explain the Master's words: "He said this to indicate the manner of death by which Peter was to glorify God" (John 21:18, 19, N.E.B.).

In those days men knew what such words held in store for them. The horrendous cruelty of crucifixion was almost commonplace, except for the victim and his relatives. It is hard for us to apprehend the physical agonies of those who were suspended between heaven and earth, awaiting the release of death that sometimes took three days to arrive. But for Peter it was an all-too-common sight. He had seen the greatest and yet the worst of all crucifixions as he watched his sinless Lord nailed to one of those innumerable crosses. Could the memory of that murder ever fade from his mind? Would it fortify or weaken his resolve to be faithful unto death? He himself provides a very credible answer in the passage covered by this chapter.

The apostle had about thirty-five years, or half his life, to meditate upon the forecast of his own death. But there is no trace of self-pity and no boastful self-glorification in the prospect of his martyrdom. He simply accepted the prophecy as a statement of fact, and described it as information that "our Lord Jesus Christ hath shewed me" (2 Peter 1:14) or "has made clear to me" (N.I.V.). It was indeed only a special instance of the general prediction that had been stated in the presence of all the disciples: "Then shall they deliver you up to be afflicted, and shall kill you: and ye shall be hated of all nations for my name's sake" (Matt. 24:9; see also chap. 10:16; John 16:2). Christian tradition suggests that many of Peter's fellow apostles, beginning with James (Acts 12:1, 2) and ending with John his brother, suffered persecution that resulted in death for several of them. These violent ends came as no surprise to any of them. This is what they expected. They saw a martyr's death as fulfillment of Christ's own words: "In the world ye shall have tribulation: but be of good cheer; I have overcome the world." And they all knew what had befallen their Leader! Yet they remembered that He had, on the same occasion, said: "These things have I spoken unto you, that in me ye might have peace" (John 16:33). Peter's message to the church members in Asia Minor was living proof of his own acceptance of his Master's counsel.

We now have no sure way of knowing the time and place from which these brave words were written. If we compare them with Paul's last testament in 2 Timothy 4:6-8 we might conclude that Peter's letter was written somewhat earlier than Paul's, for while it also was written under that shadow of death, it lacks the ring of finality that sounds so clearly in the letter to Timothy. As to place, there is no reason to reject the tradition that Peter died in Rome while Nero was emperor (A.D. 54-68), at about the same time Paul was executed. It is not possible to tell, at this distance in time, if they had each other's company during imprisonment and during the last dread hours prior to execution. Paul makes no mention of Peter as a companion in suffering, but he does state, "Only Luke is with me" (2 Tim. 4:11). Peter's reference to his fellow apostle gives no hint of personal proximity to him in the Roman capital and one of its dismal prisons. Paul may have been only under house arrest (Acts 28:30), and Peter may have been free to continue pastoral work a little longer and to write to congregations who personally knew him. (See *The Acts of the Apostles,* pages 537, 538.)

The reason for there being so many unanswered questions about Peter's career lies partly in the letter's unself-centeredness. Of the sixty-one verses in this Epistle, only one (chap. 1:14) specifically focuses on his personal concerns. The other sixty treat of the spiritual welfare of his flock. The pattern is very clear in the verse to which we now turn (verse 15).

It is obvious that the writer is seeking no sympathy for himself as he stares a horrendous death in the face. He mentions his expected fate, but does not morbidly dwell on it. Instead, he returns, with utmost speed, to his readers' situation, using similar language to that already employed in verses 12 and 13, but with a different emphasis. His earlier words were directed to their current situation, while he was still with them. In verse 15 he carries them beyond his own death, wanting them to go on remembering "these things"—those that he has already recorded and those he is just about to expound to them. Michael Green has suggested *(The Second Epistle of Peter and the Epistle of Jude,* p. 80) that Peter is here referring to Mark's Gospel, and produces some evidence in support of that interpretation. But Peter, who shows no diffidence in writing of Paul (chap. 3:15, 16), would scarcely be likely to refrain from naming Mark if he were referring to "the gospel of Jesus Christ, the Son of God" (Mark 1:1), particularly as well-established tradition declares that Mark based his Gospel on Peter's own recollections of Christ's life and ministry. And there is a simpler interpretation of "these things" (2 Peter 1:12, 13). The apostle provides the explanation in the verses that follow (verses 16-21). He is referring to the foundations on which the Christian faith rests, namely, the divinity of Jesus Christ, the reliability of prophecy, and the inspiration of the Scriptures.

In this, his last will and testament, the courageous writer is commending his readers to a faithful remembrance of and adherence to all they have learned about his and their beloved Lord.

With the Majestic Jesus

(2 Peter 1:16-18)

The pagan world in which Peter and his friends lived paid allegiance to a pantheon of gods and goddesses whose alleged powers were described by means of elaborate fables or myths. Such fictions were the outcome of men's need to identify those who were responsible for the creation and maintenance of the world. Some of the tales were beautifully expressed, but, being the product of human speculation, those deities were morally no better, and often worse, than the men and women who conceived them and the multitudes who professed to worship them.

Furthermore, since the church in Asia Minor probably had a strong Jewish membership, there may be a reference to the fantastic myths that had been added to Old Testament history. Ere long, the church also would be plagued by the spate of curious and bizarre tales spawned in the Christian Era. Saints and angels were credited with powers and deeds that New Testament morality would never accept.

From such frail sources of religion Peter unhesitatingly dissociated himself and his fellow Christians. "We have not followed cunningly devised fables," he declares (2 Peter 1:16). He employs the Greek word *mythoi* ("myths," or "fables"), always used disparagingly in the New Testament, which sees them as fiction, in contrast to all that is involved in the fact of the Incarnation. Here, then, one of the three privileged disciples, speaking as a representative of the apostolic body, announces their adherence to fact, not fiction, to a faith based on historical events whose realities were confirmed by reliable witnesses. He does not depend solely on his own testimony, but involves his fellow observers. This could also include all the apostles who learned of the experience after Christ had risen from the dead (Matt. 17:9). Some of these could have "made known" to Peter's readers "the power and coming of our Lord Jesus Christ," though the greatest contribution probably came from Peter himself.

Primary reference here must be to the revelation given to Peter, James, and John on the Mount of Transfiguration (Matt. 17:1-9; Mark 9:1-10; Luke 9:28-36). But we should realize that its significance for the trio went far beyond a fleeting glimpse of unsuspected glory. The event was a revelation. They found their Master to be the King of glory, honored by the best-loved and respected Old Testament characters, Moses and Elijah. They realized that the mountaintop experience was a preview of a still more glorious event when their Lord, in all His majesty, will fulfill the numerous prophecies that foretell the establishment of His everlasting kingdom, with Himself as king.

The hope of Christ's return was strong in the believers' hearts during the seventh decade of the first century A.D. Several of the original disciples were still alive, and some were personally known to Christians in many parts of the Roman world and beyond. In the instance before us there is evidence that Peter and some unnamed associates had instructed the believers concerning Christ's power and His second coming. The writer identifies his understanding of "coming" by using the word *parousia,* which is employed by New Testament writers with particular reference to Christ's return in power and glory. Of this, the Transfiguration was but a passing glimpse, an earnest of the royal return when Jesus of Nazareth will be recognized as King of kings and Lord of lords.

But at this juncture the apostle is concentrating on the unique revelation of majesty that was granted to him and his companions. Of this they were *epoptai,* "eyewitnesses." The Greek word originally referred to those who were initiated into the pagan mystery religions, thereby following "cunningly devised fables," ostensibly attaining to the highest earthly happiness. Here the word is elevated to indicate those who had gazed on the "majesty," the ineffable glory, of the King of kings.

Neither James nor even John in his profound Gospel has left us any record or comment on that unique experience. But they, with Peter, must eventually have shared their recollections with their fellow disciples and enabled Matthew, Mark, and Luke to include the report in their Gospels. Apart from these three accounts, Peter's is the only reference to that pinnacle of revelation granted to the favored three. The remainder of Scripture is silent on the awe-inspiring spectacle.

Now Peter perceives his final opportunity to share the inspiration he had received from the scene. He rightly remembered the Source of the glory that flooded that hilltop in the middle of the night: "He received from God the Father honour and glory" (2 Peter 1:17). Similar recognition came to the Son at His baptism when "a voice from heaven" said, "This is my beloved Son" (Matt. 3:17). What greater honor, what brighter glory, could the Father bestow on the itinerant Preacher than to acknowledge Him as His well-beloved, only Son? How that paternal declaration must have heartened the Son in His humanity! Then came the divine approbation "in whom I am well pleased." What welcome assurance came from those simple but truly godly words! Jesus and some of His disciples-to-be had heard them at His baptism. The three onlookers must have remembered the earlier utterance and been strengthened by its nocturnal repetition. Peter had treasured both through more than three decades!

The apostle takes time to emphasize the reality of that long-ago event. The three disciples had seen and heard and identified Moses and Elijah as they talked with their Lord (Matt. 17:3, 4), but then came an even more dramatic experience. They heard a voice out of heaven. They actually heard the voice. One can almost hear one of them saying, "But we ourselves heard God declaring His approval!" In the isolation of the mountaintop, in the presence of the glorified Christ, the resurrected Moses, and the translated Elijah, they heard the divine voice acknowledging the Son, and that they could never forget. They "were with him in the holy mount" (2 Peter 1:18).

Some believe that Mount Tabor (1,829 feet), east of Nazareth and southwest of the Sea of Galilee, was the locale of the Transfiguration, but that "mount" is no more than a hill. Furthermore, in Christ's day it was crowned by a Roman fort, so it could hardly have been "an high mountain apart" (Matt. 17:1), selected for its privacy as a stage for the unique Transfiguration. A more likely site was Mount Hermon, to the north of Caesarea Philippi, north of Galilee. Jesus and His disciples had been in that vicinity during the preceding week (chap. 16:13; 17:1), and its elevation (9,166 feet) was great enough to justify the evangelist's description of "an high mountain" (chap. 17:1; Mark 9:2). Furthermore, Matthew, the only one of the twelve besides Peter to narrate the event, writes of their abiding some time in Galilee (Matt. 17:22), then arriving in Capernaum (verse 24), and eventually reaching Jerusalem (chap. 19:1 ff.)—travels that would flow smoothly southward from Mount Hermon. When we meet Pastor Peter, we shall be able to ask him to settle the question!

Having said all that—and there is much more that could be said—we should acknowledge that there is nothing intrinsically holy about one plot of earth as compared with another. We need only recall the record of

Yahweh's rendezvous with Moses as told in Exodus 3:1-6. "The mountain of God, . . . Horeb" (verse 1) was declared to be "holy ground" (verse 5). Horeb is taken to be Mount Sinai, where, some undetermined time later, "the Lord came down upon Mount Sinai, on the top of the mount" (chap. 19:20). *Jebel Mûsā,* that is, "Mountain of Moses," 7,370 feet high, is generally accepted as the peak on which the glory of the Lord descended (verse 11; chap. 24:15-17). There was no natural holiness in that mass of granite. It was the presence of the Almighty that made the peak holy.

A similar condition came about outside Jericho some forty years later when the "captain of the host of the Lord" met Joshua and told him, "the place whereon thou standest is holy" (Joshua 5:13-15). Jericho and its environs were far from holy, but the Divine Presence sanctified the particular spot where the Lord met with Moses' successor.

In a similar manner the "high mountain," where the three disciples saw Jesus glorified and where they met Moses and Elijah, became holy for the time of that encounter. When the interview was over, the onlookers "lifted up their eyes" and "saw no man, save Jesus only" (Matt. 17:8). The presence of the Son of God in His divine glory sanctified that spot and justified Peter's reference to "the holy mount." But when Jesus resumed His human guise, the glory faded and the mountain returned to its everyday appearance. Only in the minds of Peter and his two companions did it remain "the holy mount." And never again could they see their Master simply as the Preacher. They knew Him to be what Peter had already confessed Him to be—"the Christ, the Son of the living God" (chap. 16:16). The scene on "the holy mount" had brilliantly revealed what an incipient faith had already dimly discerned.

From our distance in time we can perceive that under

the Spirit's enlightenment Peter was not only looking back on the night when his Master's majesty was so startlingly yet so fleetingly revealed. On earlier occasions the disciples had been visually prepared for that revelation. We can recall the baptismal scene when the Spirit and the Father publicly acknowledged the Son (chap. 3:16, 17); the drama when the sleeping Lord awoke to rebuke the storm; and that night when He walked on the same Galilean water (chaps. 8:23-27; 14:22-36). In totally different settings were the confirmatory flashes of divinity in Gethsemane, the mocking but beautiful title over the cross—"The King of the Jews" (John 18:6; 19:19-22), the postresurrection appearances (John 20:19, 20, 26-29), and the ascension (Acts 1:9-12). These disclosures must have been built into Peter's consciousness and have lent weight to his understanding of the midnight confirmation of his Leader's divinity and His eventual return in glory.

Our Guiding Light

(2 Peter 1:19-21)

Many of us as Bible students suffer from stiff necks. We spend so much time looking back at the historical records that, unbeknown to ourselves, our heads habitually incline to the past, and it becomes increasingly painful to turn them forward to the present and the future. The Great Physician and His assistants diagnose that condition as spiritual arthritis. The cure lies in a conscious wrench that turns our heads 180 degrees to enable us to look forward as well as behind.

We probably recognize that it is easier to look backward than forward. The past is always there, awaiting our diagnosis. The present is more elusive: It is always moving and becoming the past. The future is beyond our human reach; we are obliged to wait until we catch up with it, and by then it is the present that soon becomes the past. But the Creator gave us necks that swivel, and it is a healthful exercise to keep them turning to survey the complete field of history—that which was, that which is, and that which is to come.

Peter stands ready to help us in that exercise. Having taken a nostalgic, confident, encouraging look at the Transfiguration, he turns his own head and his readers'—including, we hope, ours—toward the present and the future. As a faithful surveyor of history he can hardly avoid that action, for history is forever moving forward. He recognizes that the Transfiguration is not a frozen event, fixed forever in the past, but is an ever-living tableau with significance for each believer's present and his future. It brought assurance and fresh courage to the Redeemer. He went down from the mountaintop to the chagrined disciples, the needy multitudes, the occasional convert, the skeptics, the enemies, the Last Supper, Gethsemane, the cross, and the tomb. But He went further, to the resurrection and the ascension, as the Transfiguration had assured Him.

Some of those who read or heard the apostle's words may have been thinking, If only we could see Jesus in His glory, how strong would be our confidence in Him! To such wistful thinking the apostle addresses this conviction: "We have also a more sure word of prophecy" (2 Peter 1:19). As students of and believers in prophecy, we often quote that phrase. What does it mean?

First we should note that the original speaks not of "*a* more sure word" but of "*the* more sure word," which is comprehensive, referring to all Biblical prophecy, specifically Old Testament prophecy. Although some New Testament books had already been written and circulated, there was in Peter's day no formally accepted New Testament. Christians, therefore, grounded their faith in the fulfillment of Old Testament prophecies. The apostle accepts that practice, but adds the witness of the Transfiguration as being supportive of earlier prophetic teachings—not that the message conveyed by the Transfiguration was defective, but that it needed to be understood in the light of the complete Old Testament witness.

This interpretation is confirmed by modern translations that offer an alternative rendering: "And we have the word of the prophets made more certain" (N.I.V., supported by N.E.B., T.E.V., and others). The Transfiguration, Peter is saying, confirms those prophecies that refer to the incarnation, ministry, and atoning acts of God's

Son. It might be described as the Incarnation in reverse—the Son of man being revealed as the Son of God, instead of seeing the Son of God becoming the Son of man. In this way, the summit meeting between Jesus and the two prophets plays an important role in Christ's redemptive work. It fortifies the human Jesus by confirming His divinity in the midst of His humanity, and it strengthens His followers' convictions about that divinity.

It might seem that the Epistle writer had temporarily lost sight of his readers as he relived the glory of that scene. But his next words remove the uncertainty. He admonishes his distant friends to "take heed to," or "give attention to," the body of prophecy that is theirs as Christians. This covers a larger area than that of the Transfiguration. It can include all the forecasts contained in the Old Testament and the early prophecies that are recorded in the Gospels and would be known in the middle of the first century through oral tradition, before any account of the life of Christ was committed to written form for wide circulation among the churches.

In the skeptical pagan world in which the early Christians lived, Peter's application of the Transfiguration experience was most timely. His readers were surrounded by a decadent cynicism—aptly described as "a dark place" or one that was "dry" or "murky" (N.E.B.) or "squalid" (R.V., margin)—that ridiculed their profoundest beliefs and highest ideals. The knowledge that their belief in Jesus was historically sound and was established in heaven would illumine the moral darkness in which their lives were set. Their faith would furnish them a lamp so they could see where they were going, even at midnight! Attention to prophecy and its fulfillment in the life of Jesus would provide them with a lighthouse to steer them clear of the rocks of skepticism and the quicksands of sensuality, and anchor them on the bedrock of that faith, enabling them to ride out the storms of disbelief that swirled around them. God's word, in its entirety, would be a lamp unto their feet and a light unto their path (Ps. 119:105).

The darkest night is bound to end. No matter how deep the gloom, the day will dawn. Many fears vanish, others are seen to be unfounded, and the true pattern of life is more readily discerned. To this outlook we can add the illumination that comes from the "day star" or "morning star." The Greek word *phosphoros* (easily recognizable as "phosphorus"), with a literal meaning of "light bearer," usually referred to the morning star, the planet Venus, which is visible as night wanes and day dawns. In classical times the word was often applied figuratively to royalty or deity, in much the same way as we speak of film "stars." In Scripture it is an allusion to Christ, "the bright and morning star" (Rev. 22:16; compare Num. 24:17; Luke 1:78; Rev. 2:28).

Here the primary reference is surely to the benefits that come to the individual as Christian belief first dawns upon him, for Christ is the Light of the world. Without that initial response, though it be faltering, there is nothing beneficial to follow. With it, a new day dawns, and the future is bright with promise. And Peter's use of the word "until" is forward looking. He anticipates a time when the day will dawn and the Day-star, Jesus, "rises to illuminate your minds" (2 Peter 1:19, N.E.B.). This anticipates Christ's return in glory, His second coming, which is the focal point to which so much prophecy turns. In that glorious event Peter sees the full significance of the Transfiguration.

And now, three quarters of the way through a long sentence (verses 19, 20), the writer pauses to enunciate a basic tenet of the doctrine of inspiration (verse 20). He sees this as being of primary importance. "Knowing this first," he says, referring to all scriptural prophecy. He declares that none of it is for private (literally, "one's own") interpretation. This is a cardinal principle for the interpretation of Scripture. The very prophets who delivered the forecasts were not authorized to give their own personal interpretations of whatever messages they conveyed. They were the mouthpieces to convey the God-entrusted prophecy in words their hearers would understand. At times they themselves did not grasp the import of what they were proclaiming. That did not discourage them, for they knew that their primary task was to tell what had been conveyed to them. If no interpretation was included, they were not to manufacture one of their own. God who gave the prophecy would convey its meaning in whatever way and at whatever time He saw would be best.

This illumination of the limitations placed upon prophets serves also as a warning to all interpreters of prophecy. We should take scrupulous care to eliminate specifically "private interpretation" of Biblical prophecy, that is, any understanding of prophecy that is based on personal bias. We should strive to discern God's primary purpose in formulating the prophecy. Why did the Lord share that particular message with us? What did it signify to the original messenger? What information is it designed to bring us today? This calls for a very open-minded approach to Scripture. It should lead us to search for the background of each prophecy we study, and for a fidelity to the scriptural intent so that we do not wrest it to our own misleading or that of others.

That counsel springs from the very nature and origin of prophecy. In expounding that thesis, the writer establishes the manner in which prophecy is conveyed to human beings, and thereby throws authoritative light on the nature of genuine prophecy. The statement is so clear that it becomes a definition, which, in turn, calls for close study.

A loosely literal translation of verse 21 reads this way: "For not by will of man [or "human will"] was borne [or "carried"] prophecy formerly, but [or "on the contrary"] by a holy spirit being carried along men spoke from God."

What is Peter here telling his fellow Christians? Prophecy does not originate with human effort. No person can make up his mind that he is going to prophesy. The initiative lies entirely in God's mind. The Holy Spirit is the operative agent who works through human beings, men or women, who are so utterly under God's control that they are carried along by the Holy Spirit, and say whatever He suggests.

This dictum does not establish verbal inspiration or any dictation theory, with the prophet mechanically repeating words that have been put into his mouth by the Spirit. The "holy men of God" did the speaking according to their nationality, culture, native tongue, personality, and the audience or readership they were addressing. Theirs was the language. But the mental processes, the thoughts that produced the language, had been triggered by the Holy Spirit's speaking to their minds. It was He who "moved" to suggest the subject matter, to clarify their thoughts, and guide (though not dictate in a slavish sense) in the choice of words in which those thoughts were framed. The key word in that interpretation is "moved." The same Greek word *(pherō)* used here appears also in Acts 27:15, 17, where Luke writes of the storm-tossed ship that was carrying Paul and other prisoners toward Rome. The wind was so strong that the sailors could not steer the ship: they "let her drive" (verse 15), struck sail, "and so were driven." The vessel was at the mercy of the wind. With some adjustment, the word *pherō* has a similar significance here, depicting the prophets being driven, under spiritual compulsion, to express what the Holy Spirit has impressed on their minds. But the words and the phrasing are the prophets', couched in whatever language they are employing to convey the messages they have received from an Authority outside of themselves.

This picture of the functioning of inspiration allows for the vast range in literary style found within the Bible. Each author expresses his Spirit-given message in his own way. Moses wrote in Moses' style, Isaiah in Isaiah's, Daniel in Daniel's, each reflecting his own personality and environment while remaining faithful to the message that the Spirit had conveyed to him. This concept helps explain the rich variety of style and the unity of thought that runs throughout the Scriptures.

And here in our study of chapter one in this Epistle we see the same method at work. The Divine Instructor has communicated with Peter. The disciple has received the message, has meditated upon it, and has obeyed the prompting that he write to the saints who needed his spiritual counsel. The recipients recognized the inspired nature of the letter, kept it, and had copies made and circulated. Its value was recognized, and it was so treasured that copies of it survived long after its writer and original readers were dead. Their successors preserved the message so faithfully that when the canon or contents of the New Testament was settled by the Synod of Rome in A.D. 382, the Second Epistle of Peter was included among the twenty-seven books that comprise the New Testament.

Our study of the first twenty-one verses of this letter has enabled us to meet Pastor Peter. How have we found him? Which of his many qualities have been most clearly revealed in the first chapter?

A backward look will show us a modest man who uses only ten words (verse 1, first part) to introduce himself to his readers before plunging into deeply spiritual counsel that rings true and cannot help strengthening the Christian faith and practice of those who received his message. As we read on, other characteristics emerge:

● Pastor Peter is logical. The list of recommended qualities (verses 5-8) reveals an orderly mind.

● He is compassionate, wanting his distant flock to enter the kingdom (verses 9-12).

● He is courageous, looking calmly, without self-pity, on the approach of his own cruel death (verses 13-15).

● He is loyal, faithfully preserving vivid memories of the Transfiguration as a highlight of his association with the Lord Jesus (verses 16-18).

● He is a firm believer in the divine origin of Biblical prophecy (verses 19-21).

The Reprobates and the Faithful

(2 Peter 2:1-9)

In Peter's original letter not only were there no chapter and verse divisions as in modern translations, but there was no separation between words. All such refinements were added later, to facilitate study. (See *The SDA Bible Commentary,* vol. 5, pages 115, 116.) Because of this, when Peter's scribe took down the apostle's message, the thoughts that now appear at the end of chapter 1 and those that open chapter 2 formed continuous lines of script. Realization of this pattern serves to emphasize the dramatic contrast between the last phrases in chapter 1, verse 21, and those that open chapter 2. There, two opposing groups stand in close proximity. "Holy men of God" (chap. 1:21) stand in sharp contrast to "false prophets" and "false teachers" (chap. 2:1). Their nearness must surely serve to warn the reader to be on his guard, for even while he catches a glimpse of the workings of inspiration, he also becomes aware of the ever-present danger of deception.

It has been so since that day in Eden when the Creator's warning about permissible and forbidden fruit was followed by Satan's contradiction of the divine instruction (Gen. 1:16, 27; 2:1-5). Similar situations have arisen throughout human history. While dedicated prophets were proclaiming their God-given messages, false prophets were busy spreading counter propaganda to undermine the divine intent.

Peter does not immediately pause to identify the subversives, but develops his theme and names only one of the "false prophets," Balaam, and refers to others in a general manner only. He restricts his references to occurrences recorded in Biblical history. This presupposes that those who read or heard his message were already acquainted with the Old Testament narrative, for without such knowledge his observations would hold little significance. We are therefore safe in assuming that the greater part of his readership were of Jewish origin or were proselytes well versed in Hebrew history and able to understand the reference to angelology, Noah and the Flood, the fate of Sodom and Gomorrah, Lot, and Balaam.

The apostle's purpose in referring to pseudo-prophets (one word in the original) is to use them to warn his own fellow Christians about the coming of false teachers who will undoubtedly arise in their own ranks, just as false prophets "arose" or operated among "the people," that is, the Hebrew people, Israel. We should note that Peter here employs the future tense—"there shall be"—concerning those pseudoteachers. In the parallel passage in Jude (verse 4), the present tense is used, which leads many commentators to conclude that Peter's letter came first, while the troublemakers were still future, and that Jude's came later and incorporated Peter's instruction into that Epistle.

That Peter spends time warning his readers about false teachers does not surprise us. The disciple had heard his Master issue similar warnings. "Take heed," said Jesus, "that no man deceive you. . . . And many false prophets shall rise, and shall deceive many" (Matt. 24:4-11). Such deceptions were an effective way to discredit faith in the eventual reappearance of the Saviour. Peter would undoubtedly remember his Master's warnings, given some thirty or more years earlier, and would take them as the basis for his own admonitions.

There is no clue as to the identity of the deceivers, but their method of operation and the destructive nature of their deceptions are plainly revealed. They will "stealthily" or "slyly introduce" or "import" (2 Peter 2:1, N.E.B.) "damnable heresies" into the churches. The word *heresy* reflects the Greek word *hairesis,* which had a basic meaning of "choice" and in a religious context became associated with teachings that were chosen in opposition to orthodox beliefs. Such teachings were divisive, hence the strong description—"heresies of destruction" or "destructive heresies." The word translated "damnable" *(apōleia)* in the King James Version is a noun used as an adjective, leading to a literal rendering as "bearers of destruction," with a suggestion of "annihilation" (compare 2 Peter 3:7, where it is translated as "perdition").

The strength of the writer's language becomes more understandable in the light of the inspired assessment of the damage the false prophets wreak on the church through their false (erroneous, mistaken) ideas about God and His ways with us. They deny the Lord who bought them (chap. 2:1)! What worse misconception of God's intentions and ways can anyone conceive than to deny, repudiate, and refuse to recognize and accept the Father's way of saving him from his sins! Such a response amounts to throwing God's matchless gift and sacrifice back in His face! What more can He do if we reject His plan for our salvation? What can be done for a drowning man who refuses to grasp the hand that is stretched out to save him, or refuses to be pulled into the lifeboat that has been built and launched to rescue such as he? Death comes from rejection of the means of rescue. Even so, those who reject "the Lord that bought them . . . bring upon themselves swift destruction"—"destruction" being translated from the same word earlier rendered as "damnable."

We might well pause here to strengthen our understanding of one aspect of our redemption. The Father and the Son have "bought" us! This thought is not unique with Peter: it is present in all Biblical considerations of our redemption. "He hath purchased [us] with his own blood"; we are "bought with a price," declares Paul (Acts 20:28; 1 Cor. 6:20; see also Rev. 5:9). How careful *we* should be not to follow the false teachers by spurning the redemption that has been purchased at so great a cost!

The closing clause of chapter 2, verse 1, contributes to our understanding of the fate that awaits all incorrigible sinners. They have spurned the provisions of the gospel, they have persisted in sin while scorning godliness, they have rejected divine mercy. At last, when it is too late, they acknowledge that "there is a way which seemeth right unto a man, but the end thereof are the ways of death" (Prov. 14:12) and "the wages of sin is death" (Rom. 6:23). These bring about their own destruction. As Eliphaz explained to Job: "They that plow iniquity, and sow wickedness, reap the same" (Job 4:8). Paul endorses that when he declares, "Whatsoever a man soweth, that shall he also reap. For he that soweth to his flesh shall of the flesh reap corruption" (Gal. 6:7, 8). The false teachers, who had caught a glimpse of Christ's way but had turned from it to follow their own sensual desires, were doomed to "bring upon themselves swift destruction" (2 Peter 2:1).

Unfortunately, as Peter reminds us (verse 2), the false teachers will find (he is still thinking futuristically) many gullible folk who will follow their "pernicious ways" and will imitate their immoral conduct. The Greek word translated "pernicious" is the same that has been used in verse 1, where it is translated "damnable." In Mark 7:22 "lasciviousness" or "lewdness," is used and here also immoral conduct is indicated. This prompts remembrance of many other occasions when bad religion produced bad conduct. It is even as Jesus taught: "A corrupt tree [cannot] bring forth good fruit," and "by their fruits ye shall know them" (Matt. 7:18, 20).

The evil that is done by unprincipled religionists brings "the way of truth" into disrepute. Observers often conclude that such leaders are representative of the church, not realizing that they are renegades who are not molding their conduct according to Christian standards. In that way, much harm is done to Christ's church: "By reason of whom [the false prophets—and false professors] the way of truth shall be evil spoken of" (2 Peter 2:2). Each professing Christian is a representative of the church—for good or ill. Which role do we play? An even higher challenge comes if we see in the way of truth Him who is Himself "the way, the truth, and the life." The ultimate blasphemy must be to bring disrepute upon Him who embodies all truth! We each have a responsibility for enhancing the fair name of the church and of the Lord.

The apostle has by no means finished with those who are troubling his distant friends. In fact, verses 1 and 2 are only the introduction to his denunciation of their subversions. He now, in verse 3, continues his exposé. He unmasks one of the driving forces behind their conduct—their covetousness, which makes them greedy, leading them to "make merchandise," that is, to trade on their victims' "credulity" (N.E.B.). Their stock in trade is "feigned words," or "phony arguments," literally, "plastic words," ersatz expressions that unmask their own insincerity. The church was still young when it discovered that some people were joining its ranks for commercial purposes. (See also 1 Tim. 6:5; Titus 1:11.) Such mercenary-minded individuals saw a chance to enrich themselves by preying on the simplicity, credulity, and trustfulness of many young Christians. That breed of deceivers has never been entirely extinct. Each generation in the church has furnished a few whose interests are focused on "filthy lucre" (see 1 Tim. 3:3, 8; Titus 1:7; and 1 Peter 5:2 for hints as to its prevalence). Those few are to be pitied, for financial gain has become their god. After their initial attraction to the high claims of Christianity, they have wearied of self-denial and devoted their energies to self-enrichment—of the perishable kind!

That prophecy—for such it is, being uttered by the apostle as he peers into the future—reveals remarkable spiritual growth in Peter. He shows himself to be a shrewd judge of character, a sharp analyst of spiritual trends, both good and bad. He has become a skillful shepherd of his sheep, able to perceive and evaluate danger to his beloved flock. These abilities can be traced to two related sources: Biblical history and the quality of his ever-developing spiritual judgment. His knowledge and analysis of the past have equipped him to assess future trends. He can authoritatively declare, "The judgement long decreed for them has not been idle; perdition waits for them with unsleeping eyes" (2 Peter 2:3, N.E.B.). Note the third use of *apōleia* ("perdition") in the first three verses of chapter 2. The writer's stress on that solemn word reveals his serious assessment of the damage done by the false teachers, and his concern that the faithful church members be free from their wiles.

In support of his warnings he turns to read lessons from the past. In so doing, he indulges in an abnormally long sentence (verses 4-10), which, we might smilingly observe, "peters out," not coming to a recognizable conclusion. We shall not stay for detailed exploration of its component parts, but shall endeavor to observe the application of those examples to the heretical teachers.

The writer pronounces judgment upon the disturbers by comparing them with "the angels that sinned" (verse 4). Scripture says little about such angels, but that little covers much ground. Many commentators go back to Genesis 6:1-4, seeing "the sons of God" as rebellious angels who had been expelled from God's presence. However, most Adventist commentators see that as referring to descendants of Seth, men who were generally loyal to God. In Job 4:18, Eliphaz refers to the occasion when God charged "his angels" with "folly [or error]." Peter may also be remembering Isaiah 14:12-15, where the prophet compares the king of Babylon to "Lucifer, son of the morning," who had "fallen from heaven" and was "cut down to the ground," and had dared to say, "I will be like the most High." Since we doubt that the book of Revelation had been written by the time this Epistle was penned we cannot rightly link the two, though knowledge of "war in heaven" and of the casting out of "the great dragon, . . . the Devil" (Rev. 12:7-9) might already have been held by other apostles besides John.

The weight and finality of divine judgment against the evil angels and, by extension, against the misleading teachers is made vividly clear by use of the emphatic *alla,* that is, "but, on the other hand." Far from sparing them, the Just Judge "cast them down to hell," or "held them captive in Tartarus." Tartarus was the Greek equivalent of the Jewish Gehenna, or the more modern "hell." Wherever and whatever "Tartarus" may signify, the rebels were consigned not to "chains of darkness," but to "dark pits" or "caverns," to await the execution of the sentence that had been passed upon them.

In a comparable manner, God "spared not the old world" (2 Peter 2:5), that is, the unrepentant, antediluvian generation, the "ungodly" who had sinned away their day of grace. Only (again, *alla,* the strong exception) Noah "with seven others" (N.E.B.) was saved. Peter gives him a unique title, found nowhere else in Scripture—"a preacher of righteousness," literally, "a herald of righteousness." That title highlights the issues that led to the Flood. "The wickedness of man was great in the earth" (Gen. 6:5). Only Noah, the faithful herald, and his family "found grace in the eyes of the Lord" (verse 8). That herald had an unpopular message, announcing the forthcoming global catastrophe that destroyed the world that then was. That terrible fate is used as a warning against the false ones who were defying God even as the antediluvians had done some 2,500 years earlier.

Human beings have short memories for history. The godlessness that led to the Flood quickly reestablished itself, and by Abraham's day there were whole cities given over to every known form of wickedness. So bad was the decline that the Lord intervened to cleanse the earth of two of the most depraved communities, Sodom and Gomorrah. It is believed that these were situated in the plain that then stretched southward from the southern end of the Dead Sea. The record says, "The Lord rained upon Sodom and upon Gomorrah brimstone and fire" (chap. 19:24). The Dead Sea now covers the vale where the two towns are presumed to have stood. This sorry story is retold, says Peter, to make these cities "an object-lesson for godless men in future days" (2 Peter 2:6, N.E.B.), which included those whose conduct he was even then condemning, those who were leading would-be Christians astray.

Just as in the days of the deluge, so the Lord had a righteous remnant at the time of fiery destruction. He then "delivered just Lot" (verse 7), who, in spite of obvious moral weakness, is described as a "just" man or a "righteous one" in verse 7 and as "that righteous man" in verse 8. In view of his pusillanimity, Lot is generously treated here, and is shown as weak rather than evil, and is credited with being "vexed" or "tormented" by the outrageous sin with which he was surrounded. That sin is described as "the lascivious life of the wicked" (R.V.).

It seems that sexual excesses play a leading role in human conduct whenever the restraints set by religion and society are set aside. This pattern is illustrated by the rejectors of Noah's message, by those who ridiculed the moral standards observed by Lot and, as will be seen shortly, by Balaam's fall from grace (verse 15, 16) and by those whose behavior is analyzed in verses 17-22 of this chapter. Awareness of this frailty alerts us to the dangers that beset ourselves when we chafe at the church's high moral requirements. "Let him that thinketh he standeth take heed lest he fall" (1 Cor. 10:12)! It would seem that Peter was aware of the temptations that beset even the most upright of Christians, for in the midst of reviewing past failures, he pauses to assure his readers that the "Lord knoweth how to deliver the ungodly out of temptations" (2 Peter 2:9).

The godly need that assurance, for under the stress of trial, it is easy to doubt the Lord's saving power. Peter therefore reminds them that the godly do not effect their own deliverance; it is the Lord who rescues them. He saves them specifically from one temptation, for in the best manuscripts the word is singular, not plural. Keep in mind the thought trend in this second chapter, that temptation can be identified as a call to deny God, to doubt His purposes, to distrust His directives, and to disbelieve His power to save.

Our God has had thousands of years of practice at rescuing His children from the toils of the evil one. He did not fail Noah or Lot. He was not going to fail the first-century Christians who were Peter's immediate concern. He will not fail any who trust Him now. Adapting a once-popular chorus, we can sing: "The God who lived in Peter's time is just the same today."

But deliverance for those who accept God's salvation also implies the loss of those who reject it, and the apostle takes pains to make that clear in his next phrase: "The Lord knoweth . . . to reserve the unjust unto the day of judgment to be punished" (verse 9). That painful alternative has already begun to operate. The rebellious angels were cast out of heaven. The ungodly outside of the ark perished in the Flood. The impenitent died in the holocausts of Sodom and Gomorrah. All these, and others who turn their backs to God and their faces to the evil one, must still appear before God's judgment seat to account for the choice they made. (Compare the closing phrase in verse 4 and the comment upon it.) A righteous God obligates Himself, by His very rectitude, not only to redeem the righteous but to punish the unrepentant. "We must all appear before the judgment seat of Christ: that every one may receive the things done in his body, . . . whether it be good or bad" (2 Cor. 5:10). Since Peter is writing of the unrepentant, that judgment will end in the second death, from which there will be no awakening.

Iniquitous Teachers

(2 Peter 2:9-16)

Impulsive Peter! Quick to defend the right, swift to attack the wrong, but mellowed by age and rendered gentle by love. How wise has been his approach to the troubled situation in the faraway churches to which he was writing. He knew how devastating the heretical teachings could be, yet he refrains from rushing in to condemn them. He chooses, rather, to build up his readers' faith in chapter 1, to remind them of the Lord's power to save the faithful Noah and the "just Lot" in chapter 2, verses 5-8, and to bring his letter to a powerful spiritual climax in chapter 3. He saves his censure for the middle section of his letter, and then pours out his righteous disgust at the heretics' tactics. His consistent concern is the spiritual welfare of the faithful to whom he is writing.

The ire of a faithful shepherd on discovering the carcasses of sheep that have been killed by a marauding wolf only faintly reflects the righteous wrath of the pastor who learns of the damage done by false teachers who have insinuated themselves into the believers' ranks and there spread destructive doctrines. His language conveys not only his disgust but his concern for his congregations' spiritual safety. He sees the eternal issues that are at stake—eternal life or eternal death—and spares no literary effort to unmask those whose ways are the ways of death. Let that deep concern explain the vigor of the language with which he uncovers the immoral and undisciplined lives of the ones who are disturbing the churches.

At this juncture it is well to remind ourselves of the newness in faith of the church members whom the apostle was addressing. Few, if any, could have been Christians for more than two decades (dating back no earlier than the time of Paul's first missionary journey, when Asia Minor first received the gospel, that is, about A.D. 45). Many of Peter's readers would be much younger in the faith. All had come out of paganism or a sterile Judaism. There was no New Testament; several of the books that were to comprise it were yet to be written. Travel was slow and often painful. Notable church instructors were probably few in number. Doctrinal instruction was mainly verbal. There were few safeguards against false teachings, and an itinerant heretical teacher had a relatively easy task in infiltrating the ranks of the faithful and undermining the orthodoxy of isolated pockets of Christians. The force of Peter's denunciations suggests that the disturbers were making inroads among a sizable proportion of those believers. His concern was understandable and justifiable. Its depth can be measured by the strength of his attack on the "grievous wolves" that were "not sparing the flock" (compare Acts 20:29, where Luke records Paul's fears concerning assaults against his converts in Ephesus).

Against this background we can gauge the force of the apostle's conviction concerning the inevitability and efficacy of divine judgment against the "wolves." Those impostors, who are described as "unjust," or "unrighteous" (2 Peter 2:9), might appear to have had the field to themselves, but that was only a short-term reckoning. They were being kept against the final day of judgment. (See Acts 17:31 and related passages.) Until that dread day, Peter assures the troubled Christians, those deceivers are not going scot-free, for rather than "to be punished," a future prospect, a more accurate translation of the final phrase in verse 9 is "while being punished," that is, in this life. If Peter had been physically present with the churches, he might have referred them to Psalm 37, where David discusses the problem of good and evil (see verses 1-11, 35-38). Here, the apostle is certainly not referring to eternal torment, as if, upon physical death, the wicked enter another form of existence where they suffer until judgment day.

The pastor does not leave his people partly informed about the character and fate of their would-be destroyers. He takes time and space to analyze their conduct, their techniques, and their end. An outstanding characteristic is their sensuality. "Above all, they exist for fleshly or sensual pleasure" translates the opening phrase of verse 10. One is immediately reminded of Jude's searing descriptions of "ungodly men, turning the grace of our God into lasciviousness," "giving themselves over to fornication" (verses 4, 7), and of Paul's contrasting analysis of those "who walk not after the flesh, but after the Spirit" (Rom. 8:1 and 4). God gave men and women sexual powers for procreation of children in mutual love, bidding the first parents, "Be fruitful, and multiply" (Gen. 1:28). But, alas, that gift also has been badly abused since our first parents were driven out of Eden. Lucifer has used "fleshly lusts, which war against the soul" (1 Peter 2:11) to ensnare some of the finest minds and to enslave generation upon generation of men and women who might otherwise have been "followers of God as dear children" (Eph. 5:11).

Rejection of God-given morality very often goes hand in hand with disregard of His other standards. The same false teachers are said "to despise" or "flout" authority (2 Peter 2:10, N.I.V., N.E.B.). They chafe against restraint, rejecting the high standards set by the highest authority of all, preferring to be governed by their own misguided tastes. Their predilections set them at enmity against God, and as their desires are indulged they move further and further away from Christian standards, becoming enemies of the Lord who bought them, "aliens from the commonwealth of Israel" (Eph. 2:12).

With that dismal evaluation, Peter ends the long sentence that began with verse 4! But his topic continues. He further analyzes, almost dissects, the characters of those whose stranglehold on the churches he is trying to break. They are "bold" or "audacious" in the inferior sense of the words (2 Peter 2:10). The term translated "presumptuous" is used in a derogatory sense, and is conditioned by the thought that follows, namely, they are "selfwilled" or stubborn, or headstrong. When men reject God's standards or judgments, it is inevitable that they become self-assertive, setting up their own criteria of right and wrong. Their standards are based on "I think that . . . " and "I believe that . . . " instead of "The Lord says that. . . . " Their thought is egocentric instead of theocentric, as all moral and theological judgments of the Christian should be.

Wise in their own eyes, enamored of their own opinions, these teachers and their followers "are not afraid to speak evil of dignities" (verse 10). Some would see this as a reference to the teachers' scorn of angelic beings. Others see "dignities" as "dignitaries," that is, church leaders who opposed their licentious ways and heretical teachings. The second interpretation seems preferable since angels are specifically mentioned in verse 11 and are there clearly identified as superhuman beings. This application is more easily discerned when verse 11 is recognized as a continuation of the latter half of verse 10, and is separated from it only by a semicolon. "Angels" are then more clearly contrasted against the errant teachers. The mightier, better-informed beings are more reticent than human beings. In spite of, or because of, their superior gifts—better expressed in reverse order as "might and power," possibly differentiating between physical and moral strength—they refrain from bringing slanderous or, literally, "blasphemous" accusations even against such blatant sinners as "them that walk after the flesh" (verse 10). What an object lesson for us! If angels abstain from criticizing such easy targets as those false teachers, how reticent we ought to be concerning our fellow Christians!

But Pastor Peter has not yet finished with the church's adversaries. He sees them as "brute beasts" or, as we would say, dumb animals, that exist to be captured and slaughtered (verse 12). Like animals, the troublemakers are governed by their instincts and physical needs, giving little room in their lives for spiritual concerns. The writer mixes his metaphors a little by making these "brute beasts . . . speak evil of the things that they understand not," but his convictions are clear. The disturbers are not well informed; they may have been theologically illiterate. They certainly are materialistically minded, and this contradiction—halfheartedly aspiring to heaven while being irredeemably bound to earth—would bring about their downfall. They would stumble around while dealing with the spiritual because such were "things that they understand not." Their sensuality and gross materialism prevent them from acquiring insight into the lofty, soul-expanding themes that occupy the minds of true believers. Their livestyle and debased religion bring about their own destruction.

Peter is here illustrating an inexorable principle that is clearly stated by James—"sin, when it is finished, bringeth forth death" (James 1:15). But that sad end is not a New Testament discovery. The Creator had revealed it to Adam in Eden as He introduced the wonders of the unexplored world to the newly made man. "If you eat of the fruit of the tree of knowledge of good and evil you will begin to die," said the Eternal (see Gen. 2:17). He who made all things knew that sin, in any of its myriad forms, would bring death to the creation that He had intended should last forever.

The first part of 2 Peter 2:13, "And shall receive . . . in the day time," is a continuation of the thoughts in verse 12, and should be seen as their conclusion. The N.E.B. reflects that reading with its rendering, "Like the beasts they will perish, suffering hurt for the hurt they have inflicted." That is justified by a variant in the Greek text that makes better sense in this setting. Justice is somewhat satisfied when those who inflict harm are themselves fatally harmed as a result of their misdeeds. This harmonizes with the principle that is implied rather than stated in Scripture: Incorrigible sinners perish as a result of their own misdeeds. The Father of mercies offers forgiveness to all who forsake sin and accept Christ as their Lord and Redeemer, but those who prefer their sin to their Saviour will find, as we have noted in the previous paragraph, that "sin, when it is finished, bringeth forth death" (James 1:15). "It is of the Lord's mercies that we are not consumed" (Lam. 3:22), but when at last that mercy can bring no more to repentance, when persistent sinners knowingly prefer their sin to Him who would be their Saviour, then the rolls of the redeemed will be closed, and sin will wreak its worst on its dupes; annihilation will bring sin-loving lives to their end. If that be strange doctrine, consider the following paragraphs:

"This is not an act of arbitrary power on the part of God. The rejecters of His mercy reap that which they have sown. God is the fountain of life; and when one chooses the service of sin, he separates from God, and thus cuts himself off from life. . . . By a life of rebellion, Satan and all who unite with him place themselves so out of harmony with God that His very presence is to them a consuming fire. The glory of Him who is love will destroy them."—*The Desire of Ages,* p. 764.

"They would welcome destruction, that they might be hidden from the face of Him who died to redeem them. The destiny of the wicked is fixed by their own choice. Their exclusion from heaven is voluntary with themselves, and just and merciful on the part of God."—*The Great Controversy,* p. 543.

"To sin, wherever found, 'our God is a consuming fire.' Heb. 12:29. In all who submit to His power the Spirit of God will consume sin. But if men cling to sin, they become identified with it. Then the glory of God, which destroys sin, must destroy them. . . . The light of the glory of God, which imparts life to the righteous, will slay the wicked."—*The Desire of Ages,* pp. 107, 108.

Terrible as it is, this is a reasonable doctrine. Mercy is extended to all: "Whosoever will, let him take the water of life freely" (Rev. 22:17). Only those who reject that mercy and that eternal life will suffer the ultimate penalty for the sins they have cherished. They "shall utterly perish in their own corruption; and shall receive the reward of unrighteousness" (2 Peter 2:12, 13).

In the middle of verse 13 a new sentence begins: "Spots they are and blemishes, sporting themselves with their own deceivings while they feast with you." This portrays those who are lovers of pleasure more than lovers of God (2 Tim. 3:4), and amply justifies Peter's earlier use of the word *hēdonē* (2 Peter 2:13), from which we derive our word *hedonism,* "the doctrine that pleasure is the principal good," the philosophy that underlies the amoral outlook "Let us eat, drink, and be merry, for tomorrow we die" (compare Luke 12:19; 1 Cor. 15:32). This is the very opposite of Christian morality, which has higher ends in view, subordinating physical pleasure to spiritual excellence.

But a worse charge is laid against these disturbers of

the church. Their revelings take place "in the day time," or, as the N.E.B. first translates it, "To carouse in broad daylight is their idea of pleasure." This implies that the schismatics were so debauched that they could not wait for darkness. They became drunk during the day, a practice that was condemned even by pagans! The picture becomes still more disgusting when we consider a well-attested variant translation for "with their own deceivings," namely, "with their own love-feasts." This implies that they carried their shameless behavior into the communion service, being drunk during their celebrations of the Lord's Supper. Can there be worse blasphemy than that? No wonder the apostle castigates them in such caustic language! And there is worse to come. During the most sacred of all Christian services they have "eyes full of adultery" (2 Peter 2:14), literally, "of an adulterous woman." The shameless ones cast lustful looks on women members of the congregation, ready to lead them astray (verse 14). They are so steeped in sin that they cannot separate themselves from it even when coming to the communion table! It is clear that they make no effort to overcome sin. Indeed, they have gone so far down the wrong road that they are incapable of turning around to escape the tyranny of sin.

Hardened sinners like company. As Peter expresses it, they entice "unstable souls," seeking out the members who are spiritually weak and leading them still further down the road to ruin. They were not always like that, but had become enamored of material gain. As athletes develop their muscles by exercise (Peter uses the word from which we derive "gymnasium"), so these arrant heretics develop their acquisitive skills through the constant exercise of their covetous instincts. They are bent on getting rich—quickly! This deplorable situation moves the apostle to invoke God's curse upon them. He may have recalled Christ's strong language recorded in

Matthew 18:6—"But whoso shall offend [i.e., "cause to stumble"] one of these little ones which believe in me, it were better for him . . . that he were drowned in the depth of the sea."

Here we pause for a moment to recall that this forthright apostle probably had no formal education. Yet after his conversion and the descent of the Holy Spirit upon him and his companions (Acts 2:1-4) he was able to preach with spiritual authority and charismatic power. We cannot tell how much Biblical knowledge he possessed prior to his Master's call (Matt. 4:18-22), but after the ascension he made forceful use of Biblical biographies to arouse and hold the attention of great audiences. And now, caught up in his disgust at those who would destroy his church members' faith, he instinctively turns to Biblical history to illustrate the depths to which the destroyers have fallen.

The writer's choice of illustration is apt. In Balaam the son of Bosor (or "Beor," in harmony with Numbers 22:5), he finds an Old Testament personality that suits his need. Prophet Balaam began as a servant of the most high God, and should have been dedicated to the welfare of God's people, Israel. But Balaam was covetous, and his greed made him treacherous. For swift monetary gain he was willing to curse those whom the Lord had blessed. From being the servant of Yahweh he became the paid lackey of the heathen princeling Balak. Peter's literary use of that treachery may suggest that the false teachers who were troubling the churches were also agents of secular powers who wanted to see those young Christian communities destroyed or weakened. If so, the label "who loved the wages of unrighteousness" (2 Peter 2:15) was fitting not only for Balaam but also for the pseudo-Christian teachers. This reinforces the earlier charge that "through covetousness shall they with unfeigned words make merchandise of you" (verse 3).

They were not the first, and most regrettably not the last, to use religion for personal gain!

In addition, as we need to remember, those teachers, like Balaam, led their people into gross sin. As the vacillating prophet betrayed Israel into whoredom with the daughters of Moab (see Num. 25:1; 31:16), so these unprincipled men led their dupes into similar immorality. No wonder Peter was outraged! If he had personally led some of those church members out of paganism into the purity of the apostolic faith, his righteous anger at their seduction is understandable. As a parent is horrified at finding his child defiled, so would the pastor be harrowed by the seduction of his converts, even though some were "unstable souls" (verse 14). He would find no words too strong to condemn the seducers, no sentence too severe for their treachery. He might have wished them a similar end to Balaam's, remembering that the Israelites had eventually slain him "with the sword" (Num. 31:8; Joshua 13:22). But the Christian leader was not recommending similar punishment for the libertines; he was exposing the heinous nature of their conduct, while leaving their discipline to God. Nevertheless, he did remind his readers of the rebuke that came to the false prophet out of the mouth of "the dumb ass" (2 Peter 2:16). We hope the errant teachers registered the reprimand!

The Way of Transgressors

(2 Peter 2:17-22)

Beyond any doubt Pastor Peter was deeply disturbed by those who were leading his early Christian converts astray. His concern arose from his dedication to his spiritual children's welfare, his desire to see them faithful unto the end. But he was far away, unable to admonish them face to face. The only available means of instructing them was the letter we are studying. From its contents, its spirit, and its concentration on the perverters, we can gauge the depth of his anxiety over their destructive ministry. The last six verses of the Epistle's second chapter should be studied against this background of deep pastoral concern.

The erring teachers are not merely compared with "wells without water," but are described more accurately as "waterless springs" (2 Peter 2:17). This was vivid imagery for Peter's original readers. They knew both the frustration and the peril that were encountered by travelers who came to quench their thirst at what they expected to be a flowing spring, only to find it had dried up. The grass around the mouth may still have been green, but no cool running water bubbled out of the rock and delighted the eyes and throats of the thirsty ones. Those teachers should have been channels to convey the water of life to the Christian communities with whom they were working, but alas, they had severed their connections with the only One who could supply "living water." They were no longer channels through whom the Source could furnish "a spring of water welling up to eternal life" (John 4:14, N.I.V.). They deceived those who were thirsting for the water of life. It is probable that many of those seekers were so disappointed and disillusioned that they turned their backs on Him who could have permanently quenched their spiritual thirst.

In similar language the apostle likens the false instructors to "clouds that are carried with a tempest" (2 Peter 2:17), or "mists driven by a storm" (N.E.B., N.I.V.). The imagery is susceptible to more than one interpretation. The K.J.V. suggests the well-known frustration suffered by desert dwellers. They are in desperate need of rain. Clouds appear, and their hopes rise, only to be dashed as strong hot winds carry away those clouds and leave the land and its peoples thirstier than before the clouds appeared. The deceivers were like those clouds. They raised their listeners' hope for "showers of blessing," but these proved to be "will-o'-the-wisp" that disappeared over the horizon.

We are not left in doubt about the apostates' fate. The writer declares, in literal translation: "To them is reserved the gloom of the darkness." Some manuscripts include the equivalent of the phrase "for ever" (verse 17). This points to annihilation as the deceivers' end. They shall be numbered among those who shall be "as though they had not been" (Obadiah 16).

Although Peter has, in speaking of the reprobates' end, reached the conclusion of their scandalous careers, he has not yet finished his portrayal of their baseness. With verse 18 he begins an additional list of their many shortcomings, doubtless in a final effort to dissuade his readers from following them. "They utter big, empty words, and make of sensual lusts and debauchery a bait" (N.E.B.). That double bait has proved an effective lure since the first men and women listened to the tempter.

Some of the biggest scoundrels have couched their deceptions in high-sounding words that were intended to camouflage the sensual temptations in a veneer of pious phraseology. They were trying to make wrong sound right, luring their prey into a false security that would expose them to lustful enticements. Generations of would-be Christians have swallowed that bait, and countless others are even now dallying with the same desires. This has always been especially applicable to "those that were clean escaped from those who live in error" (verse 18). The N.E.B. well expresses the thought as "those who have barely begun to escape from their heathen environment." How apt those words must have been to recently baptized Christians in the Asia Minor of Peter's day! They were attempting to live transformed lives on little islands of Christianity set in vast oceans of heathenism. On every side they were surrounded by relatives and neighbors who mocked at their spiritual pretensions, or employed more subtle wiles to wean them from their newfound allegiance to Christ.

Our author has not yet finished exposing the true nature and methods of the schismatics. In verse 19 he adds yet one more indictment that should have alerted the less-informed members of the church about the true nature of the agitators. "They promise them liberty" or "They promise them freedom." That freedom is not specifically identified or described, but the Epistle makes it certain that the apostate teachers were offering to "liberate" the wavering church members from the restrictions embodied in Christian morality. These might be negatively expressed in the Decalogue or stated positively in the law of Christ, but beyond question they did impose firm standards of conduct on believers. Those principles were scorned by the unprincipled ones. They enticed waverers into rejecting strict Christian morality in favor of freedom to follow their personal desires, with the assurance that they would then be truly free. Some undoubtedly swallowed those specious claims, only to discover that their teachers had exchanged the freedom to live self- or Christ-disciplined lives for the tyranny of physical and mental passions that made them slaves to an assortment of lusts. The truth of that assessment was beyond dispute. When we cannot overcome a habit, that habit overcomes us (see Rom. 6:16). As Jesus Himself had earlier explained: "Whosoever keeps on committing sin is a slave of that sin" (John 8:34, literally translated). It is clear that reports of the teachers' immoral conduct had reached Peter's ears, and he was anxious that others should not be persuaded into similar practices. It was not too late. He hoped his counsel would arrive in time to turn waverers back from the road their treacherous teachers were treading.

The writer has been using some strong language as he contemplates the damage being inflicted on the churches by the renegade leaders. But he well knew the *why* and the *what* of his words. Those men had once been genuine, well-informed Christians. They, no less than those to whom Peter was writing, had "escaped the pollutions of the world" (2 Peter 2:20; cf. chap. 1:4). In their response to the gospel invitation they had turned from heathen practices and embraced the Christian faith. They had done this so wholeheartedly, so thoroughly, that they were accepted as genuine Christians. They had obtained a personal knowledge of the Redeemer in His many-faceted nature and offices. This is indicated not only by the writer's use of *epignōsis* (its root being employed three times in verses 20 and 21), which may be defined as full experiential, personal knowledge, but also by the extended titles by which the Master is identified. He is here referred to as "the Lord and Saviour Jesus Christ." (See also chapters 1:1-4, 11, and 3:18, where the full titles appear, with "God" and "Lord" being used interchangeably.)

A bright spiritual future had stretched before those teachers. With their persuasive personalities and administrative gifts they were on their way to becoming prominent leaders in the churches. But they became "entangled"—another fisherman's touch from Peter!—by the very temptations from which they had earlier turned away. Their second state became worse than their first, and in their struggles they fall back into the pit from which the Saviour had earlier rescued them! Then, as the apostle perceptively remarks, their "latter end is worse than the beginning"! That is the way such histories usually go. Indeed, those backsliders were a living illustration of Christ's own parable about the man who, having once been cured of spirit possession, goes back to his sick state and becomes seven times more spirit-bound. As Jesus Himself observed: "The last state of that man is worse than the first" (Matt. 12:45; cf. Heb. 6:4-6). Now, "these things . . . are written for our admonition, upon whom the ends of the world are come" (1 Cor. 10:11).

Each Christian faces a similar danger if he allows himself to slide back into the trough of sin after the Saviour has drawn him out of it. "Therefore," applying the counsel given by the author of the Epistle to the Hebrews, "we ought to give the more earnest heed to the things which we have heard, lest at any time we should let them slip" (Heb. 2:1), or "for fear of drifting from our course" (N.E.B.). "Wherefore let him that thinketh *he* standeth take heed lest *he* fall" (1 Cor. 10:12). And a little Proverbial wisdom might be appropriate here: "There is a way that seemeth right unto a man, but the end thereof are the ways of death" (Prov. 16:25). The turncoats would have done well to remember that truth! For our part, should we not mourn that those who had once loved and served our Saviour should ever have become His enemies?

Peter now pauses to draw a moral from the sorry careers of those misguided men. As he sees the end of the road on which they were traveling, his heart must have ached. He might even have wished to turn back the clock and see them return to their first love. But, alas, he clearly perceives that they have gone too far. Those whose hearts had once been captive to Christ's love had become His enemies, with no plausible excuse for their opposition. In that case, the apostle sorrowfully declares, "It had been better for them not to have known the way of righteousness" (2 Peter 2:21), using a descriptive phrase for the Christian ethic and movement, which was often known as "The Way" (see Acts 9:2; 19:9, 23; 22:4; 2 Peter 2:2). They would then have been as their completely pagan neighbors, untouched by the gospel but candidates for conversion and capable of hearing the divine call and yielding gratefully to it.

But that state of innocence was no longer an option for those teachers. They had known (*epiginōskō,* to know by experience, the verb related to the noun "knowledge" already used in verse 20) and rejected the love that God had so generously poured out upon them. Their hearts were hardened; there was little or no hope they would ever repent. They had adamantly turned away from "the holy commandment" that had been "delivered unto them." The author was not referring to the Decalogue. He was rather employing that phrase as a synonym for the total instruction given to Christians as it came from Christ. Its distinctive note was "love"—"A new commandment I give unto you, That ye love one another" (John 13:34; cf. chap. 15:12, 17). The heretics, as Peter had learned, ignored that injunction, sowing hatred, division, and corruption in its stead.

We have now arrived at the conclusion of the apostle's denunciation of those who were trying to wreck the faith of his Christian friends. In a style that present-day taste would reject but whose vigorous language would not surprise the apostle's readers, Peter employs two apt proverbs to describe the baseness of those who were doing all in their power to destroy the Christian churches to whom the pastor was writing. The effectiveness of his illustrations is not open to doubt: they make our stomachs turn over.

The first saying is drawn from Proverbs 26:11: "As a dog returneth to his vomit, so a fool returneth to his folly." The teachers themselves would probably be acquainted with the graphic saying, and they would not feel at all flattered by it. They could hardly fail, however, to get the pastor's message. The dog was an unclean animal to the orthodox Jew, and the early Christians probably regarded it in the same light. The reference to one of its practices would therefore be effectively revolting to the false teachers and their victims.

The second proverb is not Biblical, but was probably a current saying in the first century. Even today the concept is commonly held that the sow or pig delights in filth and shows a proclivity toward wallowing in a mudhole.

Both illustrations are devastating. Without having identified them as animals with repulsive habits, Pastor Peter has categorized them so pictorially as to make them obnoxious to the clean-minded readers of his letter. He has said all that was needed; he does not refer to them again.

Unappetizing as it is, the apostle's second chapter can still teach us useful lessons. Human nature has not changed much in the nineteen hundred and more years that separate us from Peter's last days. False teachers still strut about the stage, deceiving some and disgusting others, causing "the way of truth" to be "evil spoken of" (2 Peter 2:2). Heresies, especially those that concern the nature, character, and mission of Christ, "the Lord that bought them" (verse 1), are still peddled around the globe and swallowed by the uninformed or those who are allergic to careful theological thought. Covetous Christians are already in a parlous state (verse 3). Those whose principal energies are directed to getting and spending should be warned by the judgment pronounced against Peter's commercially minded adversaries.

The fate of rebellious angels (verse 4), of the ungodly who rejected Noah's message (verse 5), and of those who turned from the witness of Lot (verses 6-8) is cited as warnings and deterrents against unbelief and rebellion. Until the final judgment day there are no limits on the reaping of horrendous harvests from unrighteous conduct in every department of life (verses 9-22). Even in this life, as Jesus taught us: "Verily I say unto you, They have their reward" (Matt. 6:2, 5, 16). Possession of a personal, experiential "knowledge of the Lord and Saviour Jesus Christ" (2 Peter 2:20) is effectual only when it is a continuing experience.

The wealth of counsel built into this chapter is adaptable to each of us. Those who apply its messages will be better prepared for the events that are described in the central portion of the Epistle's third and closing chapter.

Unmasking the Skeptics

(2 Peter 3:1-7)

If an unnamed writer were attempting to pass himself off as the apostle, he has here left a master touch of deception until very late in the letter—"This second epistle, beloved, I now write unto you" (2 Peter 3:1). The words sound so innocent. If false, if they were not uttered by Peter as he dictated his message to Mark or some other scribe, their falsity would have been quickly laid bare by the recipients of the letter.

The original readers had several means at their disposal for checking on the authenticity of the message. They could, with relative ease, have uncovered the falsity of the claim had they firmly doubted its genuineness. They could have adjusted the ascription, inserting another name in place of Simon Peter's. They made no such alteration, but allowed Peter's name to remain, which is mute but strong testimony to their belief in its genuineness.

Reference to "this second epistle" connects the letter to its predecessor, the First Epistle of Peter, and serves to strengthen belief in the Petrine authorship of the Second. The harmony between the two Epistles enables each to support the other. At the same time, we should recognize that there are no sure grounds for assuming that the readership was the same for each letter, though that is a comfortable conclusion.

The message of this second letter is more easily

grasped if the first sentence is restricted to the first two verses, instead of its being allowed to continue to the end of verse 4. In them the writer summarizes the purpose for which he wrote the entire Epistle. The abrupt change in topic and language between chapters 2 and 3 comes as a surprise. He has spent all the twenty-two preceding verses in a severe, often bitter denunciation of those who were trying to mislead the faithful. He now returns to the pacific, pastoral themes of warning and counseling his readers for the spiritual ends that characterize his first chapter. This enables us again to meet the Pastor Peter whom we have learned to love.

He begins by addressing his readers or hearers as "beloved." The term must be significant, for he uses it three more times in a similar manner in this third chapter (verses 8, 14, 17). He places the loftiness of his sentiment for them beyond doubt by employing the more spiritually significant word for friend—*agapētos,* which is rightly translated as "beloved." The Greek term is derived from the noun *agapē,* which denotes a spiritual emotion in contrast to the more social, even sexual aspects of affection that are covered by the word for "friend," *philos*. Peter's choice of *agapētos* would be deeply significant for his fellow Christians, placing the warmth of his affection for them beyond all doubt. It also serves to point the contrast between his blistering condemnation of the false teachers and the sweet sincerity of his affection for and confidence in the believers to whom he is writing.

The contrast between the middle and concluding sections of the letter may be further emphasized by the pastor's use of the word translated "now." This serves to separate the themes of the second and third chapters. His offensive against the heretics has finished; "now" he concentrates on more agreeable, lofty themes that will directly contribute to his readers' spiritual growth.

With disarming frankness the apostle declares his

purpose in writing each of the two letters he has sent to the one body of believers. He knows they have been informed, but also recognizes that they are human and liable to forget. He has therefore decided to arouse or stimulate their unsullied minds (more literally, "minds that have been examined in sunlight," that is, sincere) by reminding them of certain historical happenings and prospective events. This he proceeds to do in verses 2-13 of this closing section of his letter.

The approach is twofold. First, he bids them remember the predictions made by "the holy prophets," thereby giving a firm Old Testament basis for his message, and revealing that his readers, even when of Gentile origin, were well acquainted with Old Testament teaching. Second, he wants them also to remember "the commandment of us the apostles of the Lord and Saviour" (verse 2). The first exhortation is clear enough. The second needs a more accurate translation, such as is given in the N.I.V.: "the command given by our Lord and Savior through your apostles." This gives the teachings of the apostles, of whom he is one (chap. 1:1), the same authority as had been accorded to "the holy prophets." In establishing this claim Peter is but developing a teaching he had already outlined in verses 20 and 21 of that same chapter (see comment there). He is also laying a firm foundation for the exposition that follows, believing that his readers will accept the instruction that comes from such impeccable sources.

Peter has few illusions concerning the context in which his counsel will be received (chap. 3:3). He therefore bids his readers to face the fact that "there shall come . . . scoffers" or "mockers." Noah, Lot, Jeremiah, Jonah, and other worthies had been derided for their predictions. Christ's own warnings concerning the fate of Jerusalem had been ignored, and He had warned His followers about false prophets and their pernicious influences (see Matt. 23:34-39; 24:11, 12, 24). Peter and his congregations could not expect to escape similar conditions. They might not arise immediately; the forecasts concern the future—"there shall come in the last days"—but the outcome would be as inescapable as the Flood and later disasters.

Peter does not stay to define "the last days," so we need to discover the reasonable interpretation of the phrase in this context. In the New Testament it is always associated with the Lord's second coming. First-century believers naturally and fervently cherished hopes of their Master's speedy return to set up His everlasting kingdom. He had been among men only some three or four decades earlier, and the hope was strong that He would soon return to complete the work begun at His first advent. That hope was cherished by all believers, and most fervently by the apostles who had heard the Master's own promise—"If I go . . . I will come again" (John 14:3). But they also knew from His instruction that "of that day and hour knoweth no man, no, not the angels of heaven, but my Father only" (Matt. 24:36). They therefore cherished the hope of the Second Advent but refrained from arousing ill-founded hopes by setting a date for that return. (See further comment on 2 Peter 3:8-14. See also *The SDA Bible Commentary,* volume 6, pages 630-633, on expectances concerning the Second Advent.) It has been natural for each successive generation of believers to wonder if theirs would be the definitive "last days." Tennyson's "one far-off divine event, to which the whole creation moves" will arrive, and then there will be a generation that can check on *all* prophetic declarations and see that all except one have been fulfilled, the exception being that which depicts "the glorious appearing of the great God and our Saviour Jesus Christ" (Titus 2:13). That will mark the final "last day"!

Those who scoff at or mock divine predictions prove

to be as weak in morality as they are strong in skepticism. They walk "after their own lusts," that is, they follow their own fleshly desires. Spiritual restraints have been weakened or destroyed; carnal instincts are given freer rein. History's pages are littered with records that confirm that apostasy often opens the doors to immorality, and it is clear from the apostle's approaches in chapter 2 (verses 2, 6, 7, 10, 13, 14) that the scoffers followed that pattern. If history maintains its reputation for self-repetition, we need to be on our guard lest we fall into the same snares that entrapped those early believers. Furthermore, we need to acknowledge that weak morality is not limited to sexual sin. The Biblical use of "lust" also embraces lust for power, for money, possessions, pleasure—anything that takes first place in the affections, which rightly belong to God alone.

Immorality drastically affects spirituality. Those whose minds are filled with sensual desires are unlikely to be ardent anticipators of the Second Coming. Rather, they would view the world scene through materialistic eyes, asking, "Where is the promise of his coming?" (chap. 3:4), that is, "Where is the fulfillment of that promise?" The very question shows that they were well instructed about the Advent, for they are quoted as using the central word in New Testament teaching about Christ's return, namely, *parousia,* which originally meant "arrival" or "a being present" or "presence," sometimes being used to describe a conqueror's arrival, or the appearing of a noble personage. New Testament writers appropriated the word for use in teachings of their Lord's glorious return. That coming had become the focal point in Christian expectations and was the center of the blessed hope that nourished their faith amid cruel persecution and rejection of their message. And now they were facing the false teachers' loss of faith in their Master's return. They were somewhat prepared for this disbelief, for had not Jesus foretold it when speaking of the evil servant who said in his heart, "My lord delayeth his coming" (Matt. 24:48)?

The skeptics knew the promises; they expected their fulfillment, but were impatient at delay and not prepared to live exemplary lives while awaiting their Lord's arrival. They shared their doubts with the faithful, and for this destructive work they incurred Peter's caustic disapproval.

The teachers' skeptical turn of mind is exposed still further by their observation that "since the fathers fell asleep, all things continue as they were from the beginning of the creation" (2 Peter 3:4). In general their eyes were fixed on the present, but in defense of their disbelief they were willing to scan history's horizons to see if there were any indications that Christ's coming was nigh. They appealed to an assumed immutability of nature, from the time of Creation onward (verse 4), when God had said: "Let the waters under the heaven be gathered together unto one place, and let the dry land appear" (Gen. 1:9). This took them back to Adam, "the beginning of creation," and led them through patriarchal history when "the fathers fell asleep." The apostle accuses them not merely of forgetting divine intervention by the Deluge, but of willfully ignoring ("they willingly are ignorant of" [2 Peter 3:5]) the fearful event that came from the Creator's direct judgmental act (verse 6). He who made the world could also destroy it. He who brought dry land out of the water also covered the same land with water. The application is clear: What God has once done, He can do again.

We should recognize, however, that verse 6 does not imply that "the world that then was," our earthly globe, "perished." The writer is reminding his readers that human civilization was destroyed from the face of the earth, but the material world itself remained—or Noah and his family would have been abandoned in space, having nowhere to establish a home!

The absence of global catastrophe since the Flood does not ensure uninterrupted freedom from calamity in the present or the future. But the apostate teachers deliberately closed their minds to history's lessons. That explains why Peter took such pains to remind them of God's freedom to act in judgment on mankind.

In verse 7 the apostle turns to the future, applying the lessons from the past. Although there has been nothing comparable to the Flood to threaten man's existence a second time, scoffers should not wax bold over such restraint. The later judgment, unlike the Deluge, will embrace "the heavens and the earth, which are now," that is, the present heavens (plural, which may refer to the atmospheric heavens but certainly not to God's own dwelling place), and to our earth that had been devastated by the Flood, the earth that Peter and his readers were then inhabiting, the one on which we now live. That earth and its surrounding atmosphere is saturated with sin. Mere redecoration, even purification—and few antiseptics can match the cleansing power of fire—will not solve the globe's problems. It needs to be re-created as well as purified.

The Almighty's cleansing act, envisions Peter, will accompany "the day of judgment and perdition of ungodly men" (verse 7). Melito, bishop of Sardis (c. A.D. 190), preserves the apostle's line of thought by commenting: "There was a flood of water. . . . There will be a flood of fire, and the earth will be burnt up together with its mountains . . . and the just will be delivered from its fury as their fellows in the ark were saved from the waters of the Deluge" (quoted in *The Second Epistle of Peter and the Epistle of Jude,* p. 133). The darker, infinitely sadder side of the picture is also sketched by Peter as he states that "the heavens and the earth" are being preserved until the day when all who have been opposed to God and have refused His mercy will have His judgment executed upon them in their final destruction. This, as the revelator sees, will take place at the close of the millennium when "they"—all the ungodly, including the devil and his angels—will be forever destroyed (see Rev. 20:7-15).

This, then, is Peter's definitive answer to his critics, to the church's detractors, to the would-be deceivers of the faithful. He has unveiled their deceits and countered their skepticisms by calling on history and prophecy. These he takes to be God's voice speaking from the past to the present and the future. His survey vindicates his own position, and undoubtedly brought reassurance to his readers' hearts.

The Day of the Lord

(2 Peter 3:8-10)

Pastor Peter has shown himself well able to fulminate against those who were trying to subvert the church members to whom he was writing. Those destructive efforts had aroused his righteous wrath, and he attacked the false shepherds in vigorous language that left few of their many weaknesses uncovered. Most of that wrath was poured into the midsection of his letter, the portion that we know as chapter 2. In chapter 3 he appears ready to move on from such denunciations. He reverts to his loving pastoral style (verses 1 and 2), only to find further need for bluntly assessing the disturbers' views on the Creator's intentions toward His erring creation and the heinous nature of their errors (verses 3-6). This leads him to look into the future and see the end of such apostasy (verse 7).

And now, with verse 8, he turns away from the troublemakers and focuses his attention upon the Lord's revelations concerning "the last days," especially as they concern the "beloved," the flock over which he is the shepherd. Six times in his letter he uses the word "beloved." The first we have already met in chapter 1:17, as he recalls the divine voice addressing Jesus at His baptism. One other use applies to Paul, "our beloved brother" (chap. 3:15); the remaining four occur in this third chapter. In each case the term is applied to the Christians to whom the letter is addressed. The loving word falls naturally and sweetly on the ear. There is no suspicion of condescension; it is a term of spiritual endearment, flowing from a loving heart to a literally "beloved" people.

How precious Peter's love must have been to his friends! Some of them may have been Jews or descendants of Jews of the Diaspora, those who had been forcibly uprooted from Palestine or who had chosen to flee from Roman and other persecutions in the Holy Land. Others may have been converts out of paganism. They may have been longing for a higher religion than could ever be found in Greek or Roman mythologies, and they had been led to the highest faith of all, faith in Jesus of Nazareth, the Son of God.

In accepting that faith many of the early believers came into fellowship with those who had known Jesus as a personal companion, as a leader of a small band, a dozen strong, whom He had commissioned to go into all the world and to preach the gospel to every creature (see Mark 16:15). In obedience to that command, Peter and his fellow apostles had steadily moved out from Jerusalem in ever-widening circles. Less is known of their movements than those of Paul, who was fortunate in having an able and faithful biographer in Luke the physician and author of the third Gospel. No similar records have been preserved concerning the other eleven leaders, so our knowledge of most of them is scanty. We know the most about John's post-Resurrection history, though that is only a little. Close on his heels, as we have seen earlier, come James and Peter, with no reliable information about Andrew, the fourth member of the double fraternal partnership.

Scanty as the information is, it does permit the formation of a picture showing the faithful band of followers scattering, under the Spirit's guidance, in many directions to spread the amazing news that the Son of

God is come to give eternal life to all who accept His salvation (see 1 John 5:20). Those who fully accepted that message became "sons of God," and formed themselves into groups that developed into missionary agencies, sharing the good news that led to their becoming Christians. It is possible, though we cannot confirm the surmise, that Peter had been the evangelist who founded the Christian groups to which he addressed his letter.

The pastor wanted his beloved to be well informed. "Be not ignorant of this one thing," he bids them (2 Peter 3:8), and specifically spells out for them the "one thing," or one fact. Its importance is emphasized by his use of the strong negative—do not, under any circumstances, let this one fact escape your notice! We hope his readers caught the urgency of his counsel! Should we not also hope, and take steps to ensure, that we do not miss what he is about to tell them?

The "one thing" is expressed with utmost simplicity in English, for the words are monosyllables, apart from the word "thousand." The concept, however, is profound. It tells that the Lord is not subject to the restrictions of time. With Him "one day is . . . as a thousand years," and a thousand, or a million or a trillion, years are "as one day." That is not suggesting that the Almighty squeezes a thousand years into one day, or extends a day into the duration of a thousand years. Instead of these literalistic human notions that are stultifyingly tied to time as we know it—measured by a clock, controlled by a calendar, expressed in terms of seconds, minutes, hours, days, weeks, months, years, centuries, millennia—the apostle is telling us, as he told his first-century readers, that the God whom we worship exists and functions outside of time. We should compare Peter's phrase with that of Moses the man of God: "For a thousand years in thy sight are but as yesterday when it is past, and as a watch in the night" (Ps. 90:4).

That concept is covered by His own preferred name—the Eternal. When Moses inquired of the Lord, "What shall I say to the children of Israel when they ask who sent me?" the Lord told him to say: "I AM hath sent me unto you" (Ex. 3:14). In giving that seemingly enigmatic reply, the Lord was conveying to His people a sense of His eternity. "I AM" declares that He forever is. The French version of the Scriptures, translated by Louis Segond, captures this lofty thought in its translation of the Hebrew name Yahweh, using *l'Eternel,* the Eternal, throughout the Old Testament, as the holy Name, the God-given name of Him "which was, and is, and is to come . . . who liveth for ever and ever"(Rev. 4:8, 9).

God's eternity brings Him a stability that ensures continuity in the fulfillment of His all-wise purposes. It is this assurance that Peter is sharing with his congregations. The critics and rebels had cited continuity in nature as a source of doubt concerning the reliability of prophecy, especially in relation to Christ's return ("Where is the promise of his coming?" chap. 3:4). The pastor countered their skepticism by explaining that the passage of time must be viewed against the coming of judgment day, for which the heavens and the earth are being "kept in store" (2 Peter 3:7) and against the nature of the Eternal. "From His great and calm eternity He orders that which His providence sees best."—*The Ministry of Healing,* p. 417. Without that assurance we are at the mercy of our doubts: with it we know that our loving God is in control, working all things together for good.

Further comfort comes from being reminded of our Creator's reliability. "The Lord is not slack concerning his promise" (verse 9). The writer here employs the word *bradunō,* translated as "is slack," which occurs elsewhere in Scripture only in 1 Timothy 3:15 ("tarry") and which may also be rendered "hesitate" or "delay." Even among men, great confidence comes from knowing that promises will be kept. Without such trust the fabric of commerce would crumble. It is all the more heartening when used with reference to God as keeping His promises. It finds confirmation in Hebrews 10:37, which also speaks of our Lord's return: " 'Soon, very soon . . . , he who is to come will come; he will not delay' " (N.E.B.).

In adding the phrase "as some men count slackness," the author allows for, or takes account of, frailties in human interpretation of God's intentions and deeds. He emphasizes that apparent delay in the Second Coming arises not from any dilatoriness on the Creator's part, but from His consistent desire to give all people the greatest possible opportunity to accept His proffered salvation. He who "invented" salvation does not want anyone to be lost for want of opportunity to accept it. He possesses and exercises great patience; while there is the prospect of further salvation, He is willing to wait for sinners' repentance and acceptance of His mercy, which is "from everlasting to everlasting upon them that fear him" (Ps. 103:17).

We must diligently guard against misrepresenting the divine character by implying that He is reluctant to save and that we have to plead with Him to exercise mercy toward ourselves or other sinners. Peter guards against that misapprehension by using emphatic Greek terms for the particles "but," "not," and "but" in the second part of 2 Peter 3:9. The opposite of reluctance is true: "It is of the Lord's mercies that we are not consumed" (Lam. 3:22). "I have no pleasure in the death of the wicked; but that the wicked turn from his way and live," says the Lord (Eze. 33:11). We must ever remember that "God so loved the world, that he gave his only begotten Son, that whosoever believeth in him should not perish, but have everlasting life" (John 3:16). There could be no stronger evidence of God's desire to save His people from their sins and bring them to life everlasting! He wants *all* to "come to repentance."

We must not pass over the significance of the word "perish" in this context. It is translated from the same verb that appears in the Greek of John 3:16, where it is rendered as "should not perish," and where it stands in contrast to those who "have everlasting life." Peter's sentence construction is remarkably similar, as is also his choice of words. The inference in both verses is inescapable. God's love and His long-sufferance save men from perishing or being annihilated. In each case, mankind faces two choices—eternal life or eternal death. In both instances, the Lord's love shines as brightly as the morning star:

For the love of God is broader
  Than the measure of man's mind;
And the heart of the eternal
  Is most wonderfully kind.

—F. W. Faber

At the same time, the Creator's plans for His universe move on to their foretold conclusion—the creation of "new heavens and a new earth, wherein dwelleth righteousness" (2 Peter 3:13). His omniscience alone can coordinate the salvation of all who wish to enjoy a sinless eternity and the creation of that ideal environment. We may rest assured that the Author of salvation will so time matters that no one who wishes to accept His pardon and to inhabit a sinless universe will lose those delights through pressures arising from the cataclysm of last-day events.

With the inspired assurances ringing out from verse 9, we turn to face the situations that must develop before visions are replaced by realities. Peter confronts us with a preview of a few of those happenings. First comes his declaration that "the day of the Lord will come" (verse 10). The phrase "the day of the Lord" is not easy to interpret. It appears to be a general reference to "last things," covering events related to Christ's coming, and the restoration of Christ's lordship in the universe (compare Acts 2:20; Phil. 1:6, 2:20; 1 Thess. 5:2). In that sense, it covers a wider field than the Second Coming. We must add to this the information that it will arrive "as a thief in the night" (2 Peter 3:10), that is, unexpectedly, even when least expected. This revelation is not new with Peter. It had been given him by his Master on the slopes of Olivet. There His followers had asked; "What shall be the sign of thy coming, and of the end of the world?" (Matt. 24:3). In Christ's extended answer there was a warning: "Watch . . . for ye know not what hour your Lord doth come" (verse 43).

The unexpectedness of the Lord's return was likened to the unanticipated arrival of a thief, taking the homeowner by surprise (verses 42-44). The warning was not forgotten. The apostles must have passed it on to their converts and friends, who in turn shared it with their converts, so that Paul could write to the Thessalonians, "You know perfectly well that the Day of the Lord comes like a thief in the night" (1 Thess. 5:2, N.E.B.). Faithful Christians, then, would have been thoroughly alerted to the *unexpectedness* of Christ's return. They would readily grasp the authenticity of Peter's warning, and would read into it the need for constant watchfulness.

Yet, in spite of uncertainties concerning time and the unexpectedness of the arrival, there is a firm certainty in Peter's instruction. This is conveyed in the original text by the placement of the word translated "will come," at the head of the terse sentence. Literally it reads, "But will come day of (the) Lord as a thief." The message for us, then, is that which Christ gave to His first disciples: "And what I say unto you I say unto all, Watch" (Mark 13:37)!

Let us pause here to enter into the loving and lovable apostle's mind as he thought of his Lord's return. How real a hope that was for him and his fellow disciples! With longing eyes they had seen Him go into heaven; with yearning hearts they hoped for His soon return, which none of them at that time was destined to see. In every succeeding generation their successors have also had the upward look, hoping they would see the heavens open and their Lord returning in majestic glory. "But of that day and hour knoweth no man, no, not the angels of heaven, but my Father only," said Jesus (Matt. 24:36), so we still wait in confident hope for "the glorious appearing of the great God and our Saviour Jesus Christ" (Titus 2:13).

While the coming of "the day of the Lord" may be unexpected, the Lord's arrival is not, for the Parousia will be effectively announced. "The heavens shall pass away with a great noise" (2 Peter 3:10) or "The heavens will disappear with a great rushing sound" (N.E.B.), as of the whistling of an arrow in flight. The revelator also draws on those words in Revelation 6:14—"the heaven departed as a scroll when it is rolled together." Such descriptions depict the power that is unleashed at the Advent. To such verbal graphics Peter adds, "The elements shall melt with fervent heat" or "disintegrate in flames" (N.E.B.). "The elements" are generally taken by students of the Greek to refer to the heavenly bodies. If that assumption is correct, late-twentieth-century man has little difficulty in believing that those bodies will "disintegrate in flames" when celestial disturbances release cosmic forces such as are now foreshadowed by atomic and nuclear explosions.

It is unthinkable that such convulsions will leave our little world undisturbed. "The earth also and the works that are therein shall be burned up," writes Peter as he grasps the immensity of the powers that will be released around and upon our globe. Earthquakes are fearfully destructive, but their worst effects are often a result of the fires that follow their upheavals. As it was "in the beginning," so will it be at the end: the earth that "was without form, and void" (Gen. 1:1, 2) will be reduced to a similar state when "the great and the terrible day of the Lord" comes (Joel 2:30, 31). See also Isaiah 13:9-13 and 64:1-4 for similar disclosures.

At first sight such previews do not make pleasant reading, especially for those who take the time to let the dramatic imagery make its impact on their consciousness. But the facts should be faced. If there are to be "new heavens and a new earth, wherein dwelleth righteousness" (2 Peter 3:13), then the old sin-riddled world and its associates must come to an end. There must be a fresh beginning when the Creator will say, "Behold, I make all things new" (Rev. 21:5). Former things shall pass away, and there will be a new heavens and a new earth (verse 1). Of this there is no Biblical room for doubt. The great question, then, for each reader of these words is "Shall I be there?" To that question Peter addresses his readers in the remainder of his letter.

What Kind of People?

(2 Peter 3:11-16)

The Epistle writer does not intend to prolong his letter. He is drawing it to a close, presenting his concluding counsels and leaving his readers with an exhortation they were unlikely to forget.

Neither was his portrayal of the celestial convulsions that will precede and accompany the Second Advent intended to terrify his readers. Rather, it was meant to fortify, to galvanize them spiritually, particularly to confront them with its application to the lives they were even then living. He does this in terse language, there being only thirteen Greek words in verse 11, against the twenty-three in the K.J.V., twenty-four in the N.I.V., and twenty-eight in the N.E.B.

"In view of the coming universal upheavals," inquires Peter, "what kind of people ought you to be?" (see verse 11). The question, it is clear, concerns morality. The apostle supplies his own answer by referring to two essential qualities that must appear in the lives of those who want to see Christ return in glory. The two are "holy conversation" and "godliness." "Conversation" is an almost literal translation of the Greek word *anastrophē,* "a turning around," and was a synonym for "behavior" or "conduct" in the days when the K.J.V. was produced. Peter employs the Greek term eight times in his two Epistles—six in his First (chaps. 1:15, 18; 2:12; 3:1, 2, 16) and twice in his Second (here, and in chap 2:7)—a further fact in favor of common authorship for the two letters, and evidence of the large part that conduct plays in his understanding of the Christian life. He has also made good use of *eusebeia,* translated "godliness" (chaps. 1:3, 6, 7; 3:11) as it also is in 1 and 2 Timothy and Titus, in each case referring to piety or the practice of genuine religion, which should move in the direction of Godlikeness.

But the Christian leader is not bent on producing plaster saints. He is more interested in Christian activists whose beliefs produce deeds that enable Christ's preparatory work to be done in readiness for His second advent. Those earnest believers are "looking for . . . the day of God" (chap. 3:12), and that occupation has little to do with stargazing. They are not only "looking for" but "hastening" the arrival, the *parousia* (note Peter's further use of the special term), of the day of God. They are working to bring about the event. In New Testament teaching there is always a sense of responsibility attached to the blessed hope. Believers have the privilege of working with the Godhead to reduce the delay, to bring forward the time of their Lord's appearing. "It is the privilege of every Christian not only to look for but to hasten the coming of our Lord Jesus Christ."—*Christ's Object Lessons,* p. 69.

In the apostle's thinking, all believers should be expecting Jesus' return and should be doing all in their power to bring it about. The "day of God" is a variant for "the day of the Lord," that is, "the day of Christ's coming" (see on verse 10). It is both "the day of God" and "the day of Christ." It belongs to and concerns them both, for They are both totally involved in its fulfillment. For mankind, it will primarily be "the day of the Lord," for it is the Lord Himself who "shall descend from heaven with a shout" or "at the word of command" (1 Thess. 4:16, K.J.V. and N.E.B.).

Again, as Peter envisions the glory and the terror of the day of the Lord his attention is held by the fiery scene.

The very heavens are on fire (see also 2 Peter 3:10, where similar scenes are depicted). Recall consistent allusions to fiery and destructive events in the Old and New Testament descriptions of the Second Advent—Psalm 50:3, 4; Isaiah 13:9-13; Obadiah 15-18; Malachi 4:1; Matthew 24:29, 30; Mark 13:24-26; Luke 21:25-27; 2 Thessalonians 1:7-10. Such conflagrations result from the appearing of the Son of man "in his glory, and the holy angels with him" (Matt. 25:31). Never has the universe looked upon such a scene. The unveiled purity and glory of the celestial cortege bring destruction on all that is opposed to such sinlessness. "That day will set the heavens ablaze until they fall apart, and will melt the elements in flames" (2 Peter 3:12, N.E.B.). Small wonder that sinners call "to the mountains and rocks," crying, "Fall on us, and hide us from the face of him that sitteth on the throne, and from the wrath of the Lamb" (Rev. 6:16).

The cry that rises from the expectant saints strikes a far different note. Prior to this day they have lived by virtue of their Lord's promises and their own hopes. Now those hopes are being fulfilled, and they cannot be other than joyful. "This same Jesus" whom they have worshiped and served in faith is sending His angels with "a great sound of a trumpet, and they shall gather together his elect" after long years of waiting for that very event. Those angels are heralds who announce to His expectant subjects the appearing of the King of kings and who prepare them for that royal arrival.

Then will those patient hopes be fulfilled. The Christian can, therefore, "look for new heavens and a new earth." The old heavens have passed away with a great noise, and the old earth has been burned up (2 Peter 3:10). If the Creator's original and eternal plan for a sinless universe is to be fulfilled, the old must be replaced by an entirely new creation. That process is guaranteed in the apostle's vision. He uses the word *kainos* for "new" to indicate that the "new heavens and a new earth" will not merely be renovations of the old, but completely new creations, different in kind from their predecessors. This concept harmonizes with that of the revelator, who records: "I saw a new *[kainos]* heaven and a new *[kainos]* earth: for the first heaven and the first earth were passed away" (Rev. 21:1).

And what guarantee is there that the new creation will not be marred like its predecessor? Peter answers that inquiry in the concluding phrase of verse 13—"wherein dwelleth righteousness," or "in which righteousness makes its home." The first earth had been ruined by becoming Satan's residence. That tragedy will not be repeated, for the devil's end is assured (Rev. 20:10), and there is no danger of his being resurrected. Furthermore, the inhabitants of that "new earth" are also "new *[kainos]* creatures" (see 2 Cor. 5:17). There is, then, no hindrance to the new heaven's and the new earth's becoming the permanent home of righteousness. Of its capital city, the New Jerusalem, the guarantee is given: "There shall in no wise enter into it any thing that defileth, neither whatsoever worketh abomination, or maketh a lie" (Rev. 21:27). Instead, "the redeemed shall walk there" (Isa. 35:9), and "the nations of them which are saved shall walk in the light" of the glory of God and of the Lamb (Rev. 21:24).

O sweet and blessed country,
The home of God's elect!
O sweet and blessed country,
That eager hearts expect!
Jesus, in mercy bring us
To that dear land of rest;
Who art, with God the Father
And Spirit, ever blest.

—Bernard of Cluny, translated by J. M. Neale

The magnetic charm of that "sweet and blessed country" carries with it an uplifting, refining power that encourages sinners to enroll in the ranks of the saints. It leads Peter to exhort his beloved readers, past and present, to "be diligent," to exert every effort in pursuit of citizenship in the new heavens and new earth (verse 14). And that is not meant to be a remote, future occupation. It must be followed here and now. Later will be too late, for our eternal destiny is settled in this life, not in the hereafter.

The pastor knows that it is by grace that we are saved, and that not of ourselves but by the gift of God. Yet he also recognizes that we must be in harmony with our Redeemer's desire to save us from sin and its consequences. Hence the need for diligence on our part. We need to cooperate with the Saviour that He may find us at peace with Himself, in harmony with His ideals, with blameless characters and unblemished records. To that end, those who await their Lord's return need not only the uplook (Luke 21:28) but also the in-look, conducting an internal examination to pinpoint their most urgent spiritual needs. The standard is high—"without spot, and blameless"—the same that was set for our Lord Himself, as Peter reminds us in his First Epistle (chap. 1:19). There is no hope that we shall ever attain that spiritual height by our own efforts; it can only be reached as we "abide in him; that, when he shall appear, we may have confidence, and not be ashamed before him at his coming" (1 John 2:28; see also chap. 3:3). In this exacting spiritual pilgrimage we need ever to remember the Master's own words: "Without me ye can do nothing" (John 15:5).

The thought begun in verse 11 and continued in verses 12 to 14 can be regarded as concluded in the first part of verse 15—"And account that the long-suffering of our Lord is salvation." The apostle's extended homily developed out of the prospect of the Saviour's return and the Christian's reaction to it. Some of the Epistle's readers or hearers may have been daunted by the thought of coming face to face with their Redeemer, and would need reassuring before they could calmly confront the consequences of the Lord's return. More probable still is the thought that many would grow weary of awaiting His coming. To both classes Peter offers the reassurance that comes from Christ's nature: He is long-suffering, that is, very patient. Neither His plans nor His patience are affected by delay. He will fulfill His all-wise purposes irrespective of His followers' fears or disbelief or impatience. As the letter to the Hebrews reminds us: "He that shall come will come, and will not tarry" (chap. 10:37).

As he ponders his readers' probable reactions to his exposition of the divine character in relation to last things, Peter finds himself recalling Paul's teaching on the same topic. In a completely spontaneous manner he inserts into his letter a summary of those thoughts and thereby gives us an illuminating reference to apostolic relationships in the second half of the first century A.D. The general pattern can be followed in verses 15 and 16 in this second letter.

Peter's own written words make plain that he holds Paul in great respect as a major Christian leader. There is no hint of Petrine superiority based on priority and a close personal acquaintance with Jesus in Palestine. There is no Biblical ground for a papal supremacy based on Peter's primacy, for that did not exist. To the contrary, Peter's own writing negates any such claim for himself and exalts Paul's prominence in the early church.

Our author's comment adds to our knowledge of Paul's ministry. The apostle to the Gentiles had corresponded with the believers to whom Peter was writing. "Paul . . . hath written unto you," records Peter (2 Peter 3:15). Since most surviving Pauline letters were written to congregations he himself had visited, it seems likely that both he and Peter had ministered to the unidentified groups to whom Peter's Second Epistle was addressed, possibly in Asia Minor. What fortunate congregations! How we would love to benefit from such illustrious visitors! How satisfying will be the day when we can hear their individual accounts and fill the deep gaps in our knowledge!

From this distance it is difficult to apply the phrase "speaking in them [Paul's Epistles] of these things" (verse 16) to any specific Pauline Epistle, though his letter to the Romans would undoubtedly qualify as one example. In the meantime we can find some comfort by noting that even Peter found in Paul's Epistles "some things hard to be understood." Some suggest that the reference is to the Roman Epistle on the ground of its recognized difficulties. But others would also serve because copies of some or all were circulated among widely separated Christian communities. Such Epistles could have been read in the churches at Ephesus, Smyrna, Laodicea, and Colosse. Some of those groups may also have received copies of Peter's letters. Such incidental comments enable us to build a lively picture of leaders' movements and congregations' experiences during those far-off days!

All of the record is not pleasing. The difficult passages in Paul's letters also provided material for controversy. Our Epistle gives short shrift to "the unlearned and unstable" who "wrest" the "hard to be understood" sections. Peter's language is so graphic here that it is worthwhile to look more closely at the unusual words that he alone uses in the New Testament. The word *dusnoētos,* which is translated as "hard to be understood," was often used of the heathen oracles whose responses to inquirers' questions were so vague as to fit several situations. The "unlearned" are "those who are not instructed," "the ignorant." The "unstable" are the opposite of those who are firm in their beliefs. They are blown about by every wind of doctrine, ready to listen to any teaching that comes their way. Such characters "wrest," or "twist," Paul's writings and other scriptures out of their original meanings. The verb translated "wrest" is brutally graphic, for it commonly referred to the twisting of cords on the rack where victims were horribly tortured. So the apostle's language was guaranteed to catch his readers' attention, and to warn them against the heretical interpretations of Scripture that were presented by the false teachers.

Peter does not call for ecclesiastical discipline on those who misinterpret the Scriptures in this cavalier fashion. In this case he feels they produce their own reward, bring about "their own destruction." The word "destruction" *(apōleia)* refers to an end result that is as final as can be. In verse 7 of this same chapter it is translated as "perdition." It can also mean "annihilation," as when a city's population is totally destroyed in war; and the term occurs in the New Testament concerning those who, having rejected God's mercy, face utter destruction. (For examples, see Romans 9:22; Philippians 1:28; 2 Peter 2:1; Revelation 17:8. For related verbal forms see 1 Corinthians 1:18; 2 Corinthians 2:15; 4:3; 2 Thessalonians 2:10.)

Fortunately, the writer does not end his letter on that tragic note. In verse 17 he warns his readers of the dangers that confront them, and in verse 18 he tells them how to develop beyond their reach. But before we consider Pastor Peter's final message, we should relate his complete Epistle with the letter that was written by Jude, and this we shall do in the following chapter.

Meet Pastor Jude

(Jude 1-23)

The General Epistle of Jude and the Second Epistle of Peter are linked together for an adequate reason—each contains material resembling that which is found in the other. In specific terms, verses 4-19 of Jude's letter and the second chapter of Peter's Second Epistle, with verses 3 and 4 of chapter 3, are so similar as to establish, beyond reasonable doubt, that one of the writers utilized material first written by the other. The principal point on which many commentators differ is: Which of the two writers utilized the other's material?

A few reasons in favor of Peter's priority may be cited. He was one of the twelve, while Jude was not, and the less-known writer is more likely to quote from the better-known apostolic writer than vice versa. Peter's message refers to the false teachers as operating in the future—"who privily *shall bring* in damnable heresies. . . . And many *shall follow* their pernicious ways" (chap. 2:1, 2). Jude's warnings are given in the present tense: "there *are* certain men crept in"; "these filthy dreamers *defile* the flesh"; "these *speak* evil of those things which they know not"; "these *are* spots in your feasts" (verses 4, 8, 10, 12). If Peter died about A.D. 66/67, Jude would then be writing later when the troublemakers were actually at work in the church.

None of the reasons advanced for the priority of one against the other is decisive, but to avoid constant reference to the unresolved question, we are accepting Peter as the first writer and assuming that Jude has made use of the apostle's earlier material. This position gains strength when we consider that Jude first intended to write a pastoral Epistle concerning "the common salvation" (verse 3). But then came news of those who were upsetting the members' faith, and this made him pick up his pen, or call in his scribe or secretary, and write a white-hot letter to help them resist the wiles of the heretics. For that purpose, Peter's second chapter would serve admirably. It carried apostolic weight, it forcefully stated exactly what Jude himself wanted to say. It seemed to be a godsend—and it seems probable that Jude made good use of it.

With that approach we turn to survey Jude's message in general, and its midsection in particular, since that relates so closely to Peter's second letter.

The Greek form of the writer's name is *Ioudas,* which in English becomes Judas, the same as his who betrayed our Lord. The church has preferred to use a different form of that infamous name and has consistently held to Jude. But that name does not immediately identify the writer. He does not appear to have been one of the twelve. (See Matt. 10:2-4; Mark 3:14-19; Luke 6:13-16; Acts 1:13, 14.) Luke's inclusion of "Judas the brother of James" in the apostolic lists in his Gospel and Acts is generally taken as a reference to "Lebbaeus, whose surname was Thaddeus." The uncertain identification is usually resolved by understanding that that mention of James refers to Christ's brother of that name (Matt. 13:55; Mark 6:3), he who chaired the church council in Jerusalem in A.D. 49 (Acts 15:13). Judas, or Jude, would thus be one of Jesus' brothers, or, more accurately, stepbrothers.

It is a remarkable testimony to the brothers' recognition of the divinity of Jesus that none of them traded on that relationship, or claimed special privileges because of it. Jude observes the family reticence, and is content to be known as "a slave" or "a bondservant of Jesus Christ." Furthermore, he does not call himself, as Peter justifiably describes himself, "an apostle of Jesus Christ" (2 Peter 1:1). Instead, he discreetly states that he is a "brother of James," which probably makes him one of the Lord's brothers who became His faithful followers after the resurrection (see Acts 1:13, 14). For the purpose of our study, we accept this close relationship, and look forward to confirming its actuality when we meet Jude face to face.

We also have no difficulty in calling him an "apostle," since the New Testament itself does not limit that honorable title to the original eleven disciples and Matthias, who took the place vacated by Judas Iscariot (Acts 1:21-26). Barnabas, Andronicus, and Junia (which should most likely be in a masculine form, "Junias") are clearly identified as apostles (Acts 14:14; Rom. 16:7); Paul links Apollos with himself as an apostle (1 Cor. 4:6, 9); and in 1 Thessalonians 1:1 and 2:6 Paul implies that Silvanus (or Silas) and Timotheus (or Timothy) are apostles as he himself was.

We have no way of identifying the people to whom Jude addressed his letter. It does not appear to have been intended for one particular church, or a group of churches, and we now have no way of naming its recipients. (Contrast Rom. 1:1; 1 Cor. 1:2; Gal. 1:2; 1 Tim. 1:1, 2.) In view of our earlier comments, it might be seen as written to the same churches to whom Peter addressed his Second Epistle, or to a similar group, but at a later date.

The Epistle's purpose stands clearly revealed in verses 3 and 4. The original intent was to write an encouraging letter about "our common salvation," that is, the salvation that is shared by his readers and himself. But an emergency arose. Jude learned that "certain men crept in unawares, . . . ungodly men," (verse 4) who turned "the grace of our God into lasciviousness" or licentiousness, and denied "the only Lord." The writer does not use the customary *kurios* but *despotēs,* "Master," with no word for "God" in the better manuscripts, though the Father could be indicated since reference to "our Lord Jesus Christ" immediately follows (but see further on page 105). In view of the immediate danger from the carnally minded heretical teachers, Jude abandons his original peaceable subject matter and embarks on a vigorous defense of the faith that for once and for all was delivered to the saints (verse 3).

The defender of that faith makes a three-pronged approach to his topic. He first emphasizes the divine origin of the church's beliefs (verses 1-5). He then turns to the apostates, their conduct, their relation to authority, their character, and their end (verses 5-16). From verse 17 to the end he concentrates on building up his readers' faith, leading them to Him who is able to keep them from falling into any of the snares that beset them (verses 17-23) and to present them to God in His glory (verses 24, 25).

It is the middle section of the book that claims our more detailed attention here, because of its similarities to and divergencies from the corresponding section of Peter's second letter. To avoid repetition, we shall concentrate on those parts of Jude's message that differ from Peter's in the areas where they overlap.

We should observe that in spite of similarities, there is no mechanical copying one from the other. Even when we accept Jude's dependency on Peter, we find the later writer to be no plagiarist. He adapts Peter's message, inserts additional material, and omits some of the apostle's points. Among the more obvious of such differences are the references to the Lord's "having saved the people out of the land of Egypt" and the destruction of "them that believed not" (verse 5). Neither the Exodus nor the death of the unbelieving and rebellious people (Num. 14:26-37) is mentioned by Peter. More remarkable still is the specific reference to "Michael the archangel" and the struggle for Moses' body (verse 9). Peter restricts himself to a mention of "angels, which are greater in power and might," who "bring not railing accusation . . . before the Lord" (2 Peter 2:11).

It soon becomes clear that Peter's approach, spontaneous and free-ranging as it appears, is the more orderly. Jude pours out his disgust with little if any attention to chronological order. Deliverance from Egypt is mentioned before the fall of angels; Sodom and Gomorrah come before Cain; Balaam is mentioned before Korah; Enoch, of the patriarchal age, unmentioned by Peter, receives special honor in Jude's letter, albeit only halfway through. It would seem that, having read Peter's message, Jude picked up his pen and poured out his own indignation against those who were bent on destroying his flock, and made no effort to follow Peter's pattern, being content with having absorbed inspiration from the apostle's denunciation of those who caused would-be followers of Christ to stumble.

Jude's divergences from Peter are no mere changes for change's sake. Each difference sheds additional light on the topic presented. Each Epistle, then, supplements the other, and few serious Bible students would want to remove either from the canon of Scripture.

Having related the two letters, we now turn to consider some of the prominent features of Jude's message, those that bring us different insights or information from Peter's. For that purpose we pause to clarify a phrase that might be disturbing if left without comment. The reference is to the passage in verse 4 that says that "certain men crept in unawares, who were before of old ordained to this condemnation." This is an example of a K.J.V. phraseology that may have been appropriate at one time but is no longer considered the best. The phrases may be more clearly rendered: "Certain men slipped in secretly, whose sentence has been recorded long ago"—that is, their conduct qualified them for the condemnation already declared against any who act as they did. Their sin was heinous: "They pervert the free favour of our God into licentiousness, disowning Jesus Christ, our only Master and Lord" (verse 4, N.E.B.).

In support of his own attitude toward the disrupters Jude uses language very similar to Peter's when he commented on the angels who rebelled against God's governance (2 Peter 2:6). He also introduces some interesting variations that may be more easily perceived when set out, phrase by phrase:

2 Peter 2:4	*Jude 6*
For if God spared not the angels that sinned,	And the angels which kept not their first estate,
but cast them down to hell [or Tartarus],	but left their own habitation,
and delivered them into chains of darkness,	he hath reserved in everlasting chains under darkness
to be reserved unto judgment	unto the judgment of the great day

From this it can be seen that Jude is no echo of his brother writer, but makes his own significant changes and additions. Of these, the principal are: (1) The rebellious angels "kept not their first estate" or "did not keep their position of authority" (N.I.V.); (2) the fallen angels will not only be captive but will never escape, being in "everlasting chains"; (3) those same angels face a specific time of judgment—"the great day" (compare "the day of judgment" [2 Peter 2:9]).

In turning to consider Sodom and Gomorrah (verse 7),

Jude follows the order set by Peter (chap. 2:6), but makes no mention of Lot and does not stay to include the comfort that is offered by Peter—"The Lord knoweth how to deliver the godly out of temptations" (verse 9). Instead, Jude inserts the surprising reference to "Michael the archangel," who was "contending with the devil" as "he disputed about the body of Moses" (verse 9). Jude also passes over the extended commentary that occupies 2 Peter 2:10-14, but he adds Cain and Core (Korah) to Balaam as examples of those who chose the wrong and thereby suffered eternal loss (verses 10-13).

In his reference to Enoch, "the seventh from Adam" (verse 14), the writer once again breaks chronological order and goes back to antediluvian times. But he does so only to pick up the patriarch's prophecy, mentioned nowhere else in Scripture, concerning the Lord's coming with ten thousand of His saints, or holy ones. It appears that Jude was quoting from the noncanonical book of Enoch, chapter 1, verse 9, which was widely used in Jude's own day. The prophecy probably refers to Christ's second coming when He "shall send his angels with a great sound of a trumpet" (Matt. 24:31), or it can refer to the later coming for the purpose of judgment (Jude 15; see also Matt. 25:31-33).

The writer has not lost sight of his purpose, even when turning aside to contemplate his Lord's glorious return and the judicial acts associated with it. He devotes verses 16-19 to a further unmasking of the troublemaking heretics. Once again his language is similar to Peter's (compare 2 Peter 2:10-14), but is by no means a Xerox copy of the apostle's comments. Yet he appears to be invoking Peter's authority in verse 17, where he bids his readers, "Remember ye the words which were spoken before of [i.e., *"by"*] the apostles of our Lord Jesus Christ," and proceeds to quote almost verbatim, in verse 18, from 2 Peter 3:3—"There should be mockers in the last time, who should walk after their own ungodly lusts." But he is briefer than Peter and does not dwell on the ungodly scenario. Then he turns to the more edifying task of strengthening his readers' hold on and understanding of their "most holy faith" (verse 20), that is, "the faith which was once delivered unto the saints" (verse 3), the Christian faith as proclaimed by the apostles.

Most faithfully has Jude educated his congregations to contend for that faith. He has uncovered the evil intentions and deceptions of the "ungodly men" (verse 4), and now, in his closing sentences, he lovingly, tenderly turns his beloveds' attention to positive ways of building up their Christian faith (verses 20-23). They are to contribute to their own spiritual well-being by studying the foundations of their faith. This might be done by attending to apostolic teaching that is passed on by word of mouth, and also, if Jude's letter was written in the second half of the first century, by study of apostolic Epistles that were already circulating among the churches in many different parts of the world. In addition, they are to keep on praying "in the Holy Ghost," that is, in harmony with the Spirit's promptings and according to His wisdom (verse 20).

While salvation is never attainable by one's own efforts, the aspiring Christian is to contribute to his redemption by keeping himself within the field of God's encircling love. We are not voluntarily to wander beyond reach of that saving affection by resisting or acting contrary to the Father's commands. We must stay within His reach so that His saving acts will be effective in our lives. For most Christians this is a variable experience—we draw near to God and His love, then drift away, then return once again. Fortunately, we deal with the All-merciful, the Father of mercies, the One who is rich in mercy, counting His wealth not in cash but in kindness—descriptions that apply equally to God the Father and to

God the Son. "It is of the Lord's mercies that we are not consumed" (Lam. 3:22). And why does He preserve us, in spite of our waywardness? That He might bestow on us eternal life, "that he might display in the ages to come how immense are the resources of his grace, and how great his kindness to us in Christ Jesus" (Eph. 2:7, N.E.B.). So great is that Divinity's love for us that He needs the never-ending eons of eternity in which to lavish that love upon us!

Without pausing to explain his transition, Jude, anxious to give the saints the best possible counsel in the little space and time that are available to him, turns their attention away from themselves to the needs of their neighbors (Jude 22). He recognizes that Christian qualities must not only be cherished; they must be practiced and exercised. We are not only to love God; we must love those neighbors as ourselves—and that calls for tremendous amounts of charity, of practical concern for those in need who are within our reach. As the N.E.B. so succinctly expresses it: "There are some doubting souls who need your pity."

But pity is far too often a passive quality. We wring our hearts but move not our hands or our feet. We *feel* concern for our neighbor's need, yet remain hesitant or reluctant to *express* that concern in helpful deeds. Jude recognizes that danger, so adds further counsel in verse 23. That is obscure in most translations, because of some uncertainty concerning the original wording. But the writer's intent is clear enough. We are to recognize the urgency of our neighbor's need. We must not quibble about that, but, disregarding the danger, must run and pull him "out of the fire" that awaits those who reject salvation.

At the same time, even while absorbed in rescue operations, we need to guard against being contaminated by close contact with sin. The Saviour's example can help us there. During His stay among us He came in daily contact with evil, yet remained "without blemish and without spot" (1 Peter 1:19). Part of the reason for His blameless record is His abhorrence of sin—of Him, the Father declared in terms of Psalm 45:7, "Thou hast loved righteousness, and hated iniquity" (Heb. 1:9). Those who wish to cooperate with Christ in saving others from sin must share in a similar hatred of iniquity. Jude expresses that requirement by urging us to hate "even the garment spotted by the flesh" (Jude 23). The word he uses for "garment" is *chitōn,* which is defined as a "tunic or shirt, a garment worn next to the skin, and by both sexes." This shows an awareness of the insidious danger of contamination by contact, a danger against which even the most godly must guard. They who wish to remain "unspotted from the world" must be circumspect, abstaining "from all appearance of evil."

With those closing exhortations Jude brings his urgently written letter within sight of its conclusion. In response to news of the schismatics, and under the Spirit's guidance, he has given his "beloved" the best counsel he can pour into a relatively brief letter. (Contrast its single chapter with Romans 1-16, 1 Corinthians 1-16, Hebrews 1-13, and Revelation 1-22.) Into its small bottle he has poured a rich mixture of factual advice that bears most explicitly on the situation that is disturbing his Christian friends.

By a miracle of preservation that counsel lies before us today, "written for our admonition, upon whom the ends of the world are come," as Paul might say (1 Cor. 10:11). After more than nineteen hundred years the words of Jude's Epistle can still encourage millions of Christians throughout a much wider world than Jude ever conceived. Our study of its salient features should have convinced us of its spiritual values, and have made a home for its wisdom in our receptive hearts.

Its crowning beauty, verses 24 and 25, is being kept for deeper study in company with Peter's conclusion to his second letter. To that study, with our parting glance focused particularly on Peter and his advice, we turn in our concluding chapter.

Goodbye, Pastors Jude and Peter!

(Jude 24, 25; 2 Peter 3:17, 18)

Many of us who read these words are concluding a three-month visit with Pastor Peter. We have become better acquainted with that dynamic disciple, having come face to face with a mature, dedicated, unselfish leader whose principal concern has been the welfare of his distant parishioners. It is not easy to say goodbye to such a friend, so we shall postpone the farewell for a page or two, while we spend a few more paragraphs with the Lord's brother Jude.

We have found Jude's personality to be no less appealing than those of his fellow evangelists. He shows a similar breadth of character that enables him, a Galilean Jew from Nazareth, to reach out effectively to guide a cosmopolitan group of converts in a Roman province, possibly in Asia Minor. He exercises strong spiritual authority over them, as we see in the stern counsel he gives concerning their relation to false teachers (Jude 4-19). He must also have gained their affection as well as respect, for he three times calls them "beloved" (verses 3, 17, 20). That mode of address is fully justified by the loving counsel he gives them both before (verse 3) and after (verses 20-23) his exposé of the apostates.

Jude's spiritual stature is nowhere better revealed than in the words that bring his urgent and hurried pastoral letter to its close (verses 24, 25). That doxology, and doxology it is since its clear purpose is to give glory *(doxa)* to God, stands out as one of the highlights in New Testament literature. Its beauty shines splendidly in the K.J.V., which faithfully conveys the intent of the original and needs only minor adjustments at the hand of modern textual scholarship.

Each phrase in this sublime doxology calls for the closest, deepest, and highest consideration we can give it. The initial word "now" is needed both as a separation from the preceding human concerns, and as an introduction to the sublimities of Godhood that immediately follow. That separation accomplished, the writer introduces the Eternal in terms that immediately commend Him to us who daily struggle against temptation. He "is able to keep you from falling" is Jude's description (verse 24). He has the power (*dunamis*—from which we get our word "dynamite"—strength, might, ability) to keep or preserve us as Christians who do not stumble into sin. This brings immediate assurance to those who are daily beset by many pitfalls. The promise and the fact of support were based on Jude's own experience and on Scripture (Isa. 43:2; compare John 15:5).

The apostle, for such Jude was, is not content with a negative work—that we should be kept from stumbling into sin. His eyes are raised much higher. He looks up to the day when our God, who has here kept or guarded us from irretrievably falling into sin, shall "present" or "make us to stand" in the presence of His glory. That is an awe-inspiring prospect. He before whom the angels veil their faces, He who explained to Moses, "Thou canst not see my face: for there shall no man see me, and live" (Ex. 33:20)—He, the All-Holy, is going to set us before His own sinless self. And that is to be no momentary presentation. He plans to place us there permanently, once and for all. That can be done only for those who are "faultless" or "unblemished," "blameless."

And who are they? ready-made saints? supermen,

superwomen? No. They are everyday sinners who by their Saviour's grace and power have been kept from falling into or continuing in sin. They are men and women who, thanks to the Redeemer's influence and enabling power, have turned from sin and accepted the Saviour from sin as their Master and Lord. His name is "JESUS: for he shall save his people from their sins" (Matt. 1:21). Thanks to His faultless life, death, resurrection, and eternal priesthood, they can stand faultless before the One in whose presence the angels veil their faces. The Father, who only has immortality, who dwells in light that no man can approach unto, sees repentant sinners through the person of His sinless Son, through whom their sins are forgiven and by whom they are transformed into new creatures.

Small wonder, then, that Jude describes the redeemed as being presented before heaven's Majesty "with exceeding great joy"—the added word "great" being implied in the one Greek word since the term refers to the greatest possible rejoicing. Try as we may, we cannot here conceive the ecstasy that will flood our hearts when, with all fear of falling into sin removed, and with death, that last dread enemy, destroyed, we stand faultless before "the King eternal, immortal, invisible, the only wise God" (1 Tim. 1:17).

Although our most vivid imaginings fall far short of the promised reality, we can discern enough to fill our hearts with inexpressible gratitude for the One who so loved us that He made it possible for us to share that eternal, sinless glory with Him. To Him, "the only wise God our Saviour," we, with Jude, gratefully ascribe "glory and majesty, dominion and power, both now and ever" (Jude 25). The ascription assures us of the dependability of that heavenly prospect. Its Architect is "the only wise God" who has made Himself our Saviour. To Him, even now, we can give our measure of gratitude, devotion, and praise.

Later, when "the kingdoms of this world are become the kingdoms of our Lord, and of his Christ," we shall be able to join with "every creature which is in heaven, . . . saying, Blessing, and honour, and glory, and power, be unto him that sitteth upon the throne, and unto the Lamb for ever and ever" (Rev. 11:15; 5:13).

And so we come to Pastor Peter's farewell (2 Peter 3:17, 18).

By any modern measure Peter's Second Epistle has been a long letter. He has dealt with many topics—spiritual development, the reliability of prophecy (chapter 1); the deceptive doctrines of false teachers (chapter 2); the certainties of Christ's coming, the need for steadfastness while awaiting the Advent, the urgency of being morally and spiritually ready for the Lord's appearing (chapter 3). The Epistle's two final verses now warn against apostasy (verse 17) and urge continual growth in our relations with the Master (verse 18). Those closing messages call for more detailed attention.

In the course of writing his letter, the apostle has introduced a full cast of Biblical personalities. The first, the most mentioned and the most illustrious, far beyond comparison with any others, are God the Father and our Saviour Jesus Christ (chap. 1:1). Then, in order of appearance, come Noah, Lot, Balaam, holy prophets, apostles, scoffers, the fathers, and Paul. But at the center of his concern there are "them that have obtained like precious faith with us" (chap. 1:1), his readers whom he four times addresses in chapter 3 as his "beloved" (verses 1, 8, 14, 17). They are the reason for the Epistle. It is to them that he now returns as he concludes his message.

The writer focuses his readers' attention on themselves by his emphatic use of the personal pronoun "ye" or "you," giving it first place in the sentence (verse 17) and thereby emphasizing his intense concern for them. He also conveys his confidence in their understanding of the disturbers' wiles: these they have already recognized. At the same time, he wants them to be on their guard—"guard yourselves," he says—lest they be led astray or carried away by the deceptive teachings of the lawless ones. If that should happen, they would tumble from the firm position they were then occupying.

Throughout Scripture the warning is sounded: "Let him that thinketh he standeth take heed lest he fall" (1 Cor. 10:12). "Let us be careful not to neglect the danger signals and the warnings given in His Word. Unless heed is given to these warnings, and defects of character are overcome, those defects will overcome those who possess them, and they will fall into error, apostasy, and open sin. The mind that is not elevated to the highest standard will in time lose its power to retain that which it had once gained."—*Testimonies,* vol. 5, p. 537. Peter had great confidence in the spiritual stability of his readers, but he also wanted them to recognize that they would endanger their safety if they did not remain vigilant for truth and resistant to error.

How could he help his loyal friends to be steadfast? His entire letter is an extended response to that question. This is illustrated at the close of his "ladder" where he declares, "If ye do these things, ye shall never fall" (2 Peter 1:10). If his readers, ancient and modern, go on developing the Christian virtues, from faith to love (verses 5-7), they will develop such close connections with their Saviour that they will never backslide. How can they and we ensure such development? Peter answers that practical question in the closing verse of this eminently practical Epistle. His counsel is as valid today as it was when the apostle first expressed it.

He tells us to "grow," or "increase" (chap. 3:18). Growth is necessary for life. The puppy, the kitten, the plant, or the child that does not grow will die. The Christian who has experienced the new birth by being born again must grow in Christian stature or he will remain a spiritual dwarf and be unfit for the kingdom to come. Realizing this, the apostle bids us to keep on growing, never stopping, always adding to the Christlikeness of character that first inspired us to follow the Sinless One.

The area of growth is distinctly stated. First, we are to "grow in grace." That requires that we have an understanding of the meaning of "grace." What is it? It is possible to get lost in a study of "grace" as it is used by Paul in his Epistles, but that would divert our attention from Peter's use of the word. He is clearly writing of a quality that we can possess, and in which we can grow or increase. But as the hymn says, "I have no strength or goodness, no wisdom of my own"(from *"I Could Not Do Without Thee,"* Frances Ridley Havergal); and no "grace," either! Where, then, does that leave us? How can we grow in a quality that we do not possess? God comes to our rescue. Grace "is the gift of God" (Eph. 2:8), a gift that we must allow to function in our lives that we might become more Godlike. As it was with Jesus, so it may be with us: "And the child grew, and waxed strong in spirit, filled with wisdom: and the grace of God was upon him" (Luke 2:40). He who is still our exemplar enables us to emulate His own perfect example by growing in the Christian graces that were so perfectly displayed in His sinless life. In this setting we can define growth in grace as being growth in Christlikeness, and that, by definition, is what Christianity is all about!

That sounds very lofty, beautiful, and attractive—but how can it take place in our own lives? Peter provides the answer to that question, too. He bids us also to grow "in the knowledge of our Lord and Saviour Jesus Christ" (2 Peter 3:18). It is tempting to wish that he had used the same word, *epignōsis,* that full experiential knowledge, as he did in chapters 1:2, 3, 8 and 2:20; but he did not, so we must content ourselves with growth in our acquaintanceship with Jesus. If we pursue that diligently it will lead to no less rich a knowledge than the more intensive type of which Paul says so much and with which Peter is also clearly acquainted. That can result in endless growth, here and in eternity.

When all is said and done, how can we distinguish between levels or types of knowledge of the all-glorious Lord Jesus? The newly converted can, in his or her own way, love the Saviour as ardently as the most mature Christian, though not possessing the same depth and experience of that knowledge. Perhaps, then, it is well that the writer used the more usual word for knowledge when exhorting us to grow in that knowledge of our Lord and Saviour Jesus Christ.

While contemplating ever-increasing growth in our personal acquaintance with and loyalty to our Redeemer, we ought reverently to ensure whom we are seeking to know. He is "our Lord and Saviour Jesus Christ" (chap. 3:18). That makes us His subjects, and Him our sovereign. He is also our Saviour, the one who has redeemed us, who has bought us with His own blood. At the same time He is our Elder Brother Jesus, the Divine-Human Person who came to Bethlehem and endured the drab sinfulness of Nazareth, being "made like unto his brethren, . . . to make reconciliation for the sins of the people" (Heb. 2:17). He is also the Christ, Messiah, the Anointed One who is the King of kings and Lord of lords, the One who will reign "for ever and ever" (see Rev. 11:15). It should not be difficult for us to give Him "glory both now and for ever." If we sincerely do that here in our workaday world, we shall be among those who will continue doing it for ever and ever, for, as we studied from chapter 1:3 and 4, "his divine power hath given unto us all things that pertain unto life and godliness . . . that by these ye might be partakers of the divine nature," and that nature is eternal.

Epilogue

If Peter were to meet us today he might well want to compare us with those earlier friends of his who lived under much harsher conditions than most of us have ever been asked to endure. How do we, living as comfortably as most of us do, measure up to the standards set for those who want to share in the divine nature? We ourselves can provide quite a comprehensive answer, drawn from the apostle's own concluding words in this third chapter of Second Peter.

Question. What kind of people ought we to be?

Answer. People who live holy and godly lives (verse 11).

Q. How should we be occupied?

A. Anticipating and expediting "the coming of the day of God" (verse 12).

Q. For what specific revelations should we look?

A. "New heavens and a new earth" (verse 13).

Q. How may we hasten the arrival of this new universe?

A. By diligent service and blameless living (verse 14), and being on our guard against personal apostasy (verse 17).

Q. How should we employ our waiting time?

A. By growth in Christian graces and personal knowledge of our Lord and Saviour (verse 18).

Au Revoir, Pastor Peter

We are glad to have met you, Pastor Peter. We believe we shall recognize you when we meet again, thanks to the portrait that peeps out from the Gospels and your own two letters. We hope the reunion comes soon!

We shall look for the leading disciple, a Galilean, stalwart, moderately tall, matured by hardship and responsibility, kindly faced, the shepherd who cares for the lambs as well as the sheep. Yes, we know "we shall all be changed," but not beyond recognition. We shall stand on the sidelines and watch for the trio who saw their Master glorified on the mountaintop, and we shall greet James and John while trying to draw closer still to the one and only Peter. With him we shall await the daydawn and the Day-star, and shall see prophecy reach its zenith as the Lord Himself appears.

We shall look for the servant and apostle of Jesus Christ, for him who cared for many of those who had obtained like precious faith with other early believers. We shall seek the spiritual counselor who fortified the embattled saints as they struggled to stay firm in the faith while they were being bitterly persecuted, and while false teachers were trying to weaken their loyalty to their Lord.

We shall look for the disciple who had humbly but confidently declared to the Resurrected One, "Lord, thou knowest all things; thou knowest that I love thee" (John 21:17), and had proved that by bravely embracing the cruelty of the cross as the fulfillment of his Master's forecast of his death.

We shall heed the pastor's warnings against impostor prophets, and help others to stay clear of their toils. We shall draw on Scripture to discern between the true and the false in prophetic interpretation, and bring each identification to the touchstone of truth, asking how each harmonizes with the Lord's own revelation of His nature and His modes of working within human history. We shall take Peter's additional information concerning last things and fit it into the total Biblical picture, especially noting his understanding of "the day of God" that will raise the curtain on the "new heavens and a new earth."

We shall respond to the apostolic counsel "Be diligent. . . . Beware. . . . Grow in grace, and in the knowledge of our Lord and Saviour Jesus Christ" (2 Peter 3:14-18). While growing, we shall also prepare to join with Peter, his companion apostles, and all the countless host of believers who will join in ascribing to their blessed Redeemer "glory both now and for ever. Amen" (verse 18).

O then what raptured greetings
  On Canaan's happy shore!
What knitting severed friendship where
  Death partings are no more!
Then eyes with joy shall sparkle,
  That brimmed with tears of late;
Orphans no longer fatherless,
  Nor widows desolate.

Bring near Thy great salvation,
  Thou Lamb for sinners slain,
Fill up the roll of Thine elect,
  Then take Thy power and reign!
Appear, Desire of nations,
  Thine exiles long for home;
Show in the heavens Thy promised sign;
  Thou Prince and Saviour, come!

—Henry Alford

Thank you, Pastor Peter. Please be sure to watch for us at the coming of the day of God, for we do want to meet you, face to face.